Defending Animals' Rights

IS THE

RIGHT THING TO DO

Defending Animals' Rights
IS THE
RIGHT THING TO DO

B. P. ROBERT STEPHEN SILVERMAN, Ph.D.

s.p.i.
BOOKS

To my mother,
Clara Lavenstein Silverman—
a woman of courage and compassion...
And in memory of my father,
Abraham George (Al) Silverman—
a strong man who was always gentle

S.P.I. BOOKS

A division of Shapolsky Publishers, Inc.

Copyright © 1992 by B. P. Robert Stephen Silverman

For any additional information, contact:

Shapolsky Publishers, Inc.
136 West 22nd Street
New York, NY 10011
(212) 633-2022
FAX (212) 633-2123

10 9 8 7 6 5 4 3 2 1

Library of Congress Cataloging-in-Publication Data

Silverman, B. P. Robert Stephen, 19–
    Defending animals' rights is the right thing to do / by B. P.
Robert Stephen Silverman
        p.   cm.
    Includes bibliographical references.
    ISBN 1-56171-044-X (softcover)
    1. Animal rights.   2. Animal welfare—United States.   I. Title.
HV4708.S55   1991
179'.3—dc20   91-12396

Design and Typography by Smith, Inc., New York
Manufactured in the United States of America

*"I always had a deep, instinctive understanding
of animals, a yearning to hold them in my arms,
a fierce desire to protect them against pain and cruelty.
. . . I felt that I* knew things about them—*their
sensations, desires and sensibilities—that other bipeds
could not guess; and this seemed to lay on me the
obligation to defend them against their human
oppressors."*

"[I see] the usness *in their eyes, with the underlying*
not-us*ness which belies it, and is so tragic a reminder
of the lost age when we human beings branched off
and left them: left them to inarticulateness and slavery.
Why? their eyes seem to ask us."*

—Edith Wharton, "Life and I"
and "Quaderno dello Studente," respectively,
Wharton Archives, Yale University

———————————

"It should not be a question simply of how they
should be treated within the context of their usefulness,
or perceived usefulness, to us, but rather whether
we have a right to use them at all."

—Ingrid Newkirk
in *Save the Animals!
101 Easy Things You Can Do*

Acknowledgments

Thanks go to *The Animals' Agenda* for contributing their compilation of financial information on animal charities (Appendix C) and for publishing my request to correspond with activists, not to mention the more than one hundred activists who collectively shared their personal philosophies on animals' rights. Dr. Martha Gagnon provided the inspiration for the title of this book. Gale Research, Inc., contributed the comprehensive directory of animal associations (Appendix A). The groups People for the Ethical Treatment of Animals, the Farm Animal Reform Movement, and the National Alliance for Animal Legislation provided a wide selection of photographs; and an anonymous London contributor sent me exclusive photographs showing the underground Animal Liberation Front in action. In addition, there are six individuals who personally shaped my philosophy on animals' rights: Ingrid Newkirk, Alex Pacheco, Dr. Neal Barnard, Dr. Alex Hershaft, Grace Slick, and Rabbi Harold S. White. Thank you all very much.

Finally, this book would have been impossible without the love and support of my "co-authors," my senior citizen companion animals Lady Pompie and Cappuccino, who sat beside me as I wrote it. Tragically, Cappuccino could not be here to see its completion.

Contents

"Good intentions are not enough" is the motto of PETA National
Director Ingrid Newkirk. As her work guides the animal-rights
movement into the mainstream, Ingrid has found that professional
work that other compassionate people do can be a valuable resource.
In her *Save the Animals!* she names a produce store owner who
donates food to a sanctuary for homeless animals, an ophthalmologist
who gives expert testimony against eye-irritancy tests on rabbits, a
carpenter who builds booths for animals groups, and a trucking
company that distributes animal-rights literature with every drop-off.
Undoubtedly, it is she who inspired them.
(Photo courtesy of PETA)

Foreword

by Ingrid Newkirk

*B*uddy Silverman is a thinker. He is also an empathetic person who argues the case for animals' rights forthrightly and without pulling any punches. He has written a hard-hitting, well-referenced book full of historical parallel, uncomfortably current photographs, and solid arguments that challenge people—whether they care about animals or do not—to be consistent in their reasoning. He even provides simple exercises to help us understand what motivates us to protect animals, or why we deny them respect. At least the exercises *seem* simple, but are they really? What they reveal cannot only help us gauge our commitment to animal rights, or lack of it, but can help us recognize some of the inhibitions and reservations, even the mythology, that may be holding us back from being morally responsible citizens.

It should be apparent from Dr. Silverman's writing that he is someone who not only wrestles with what is right and wrong to do to others, regardless of their race, color, gender, or species, but lives what he believes. His own heartbreaks, guilt over past behaviors, and moral evolution are spelled out on these pages. His own deductions and experiences are well mixed with the remarks or excerpts from the writings of the physician Roy Kupsinel, who disproves the myth of animal research having value, and philosopher Peter Singer, who reminds us that " 'species-ism,' by analogy with racism, must also be condemned."

Hunters, experimenters, furriers, and fur-wearers will have good cause to be angry at Dr. Silverman, because *Defending Animals' Rights Is the Right Thing to Do* will certainly change forever the way readers think about animals.

Ingrid Newkirk
National Director, People for
the Ethical Treatment of Animals
and
author of *Save the Animals!*
101 Easy Things You Can Do
and *Kids Can Save the Animals!*

A Word on Animal Genocide and the Holocaust

*I*n this book, I draw an analogy between animal genocide committed by Americans today and human genocide committed by Germans more than a half-century ago. Nothing that has ever happened is as tragic as was the Holocaust. I have read verified accounts of the Holocaust that are too grotesque to recount; and I have seen Holocaust photographs that are too grotesque to exhibit.

I will never forget one particular photograph of a Jewish woman, who was identified in the caption as having come from Langenau, near. Bromberg. The caption to that photograph is indelible in my mind—perhaps even more indelible than the photograph, which is grotesque beyond words. The caption states that her right foot was hacked off, then the leg was severed from the thigh in butcher fashion. Is it not clear that brutality to animals can encourage such crimes against humanity?

It is important to recognize that animals anticipate and feel pain in the same way as humans, even though it is difficult for us to relate readily to suffering experienced by non-humans. Nevertheless, the pain is the same; only the species has changed.

Drawing an analogy between the atrocities inflicted upon human beings and the atrocities inflicted upon animals does not diminish our concern for human victims. It is no insult to compare acts that result in collective suffering, regardless of whether the suffering was experienced by Jewish people in concentration camps, African-Americans as slaves, or animals in laboratories. The results, though not the victims, are the same.

B. P. Robert Stephen Silverman, Ph.D.
1991

Introduction

*U*gandan President Idi Amin sent chills up the spines of civilized people during the 1970s when he bragged about having practiced cannibalism, and as recently as July 1991, cannibalism was reported to have been committed in the United States by mass murderer Jeffrey L. Dahmer. But is it not also unsettling to consider the implications of a typical American eating a piece of fried chicken? It is certainly unsettling to reflect upon the mad ravings of Ed Gein, the real-life inspiration for Alfred Hitchcock's Norman Bates in the movie "Psycho." According to Gein, the tastes of human flesh and chicken were "very much the same." Is it not also unsettling to know that the pain chickens suffer is the same?

Civilized people reacted with shock during the 1940s over revelations about Nazi doctor Josef Mengele. He had tortured countless humans to death in diabolical medical experiments. But were not Mengele's atrocities a gruesome extension of the experiments still performed on animals in the United States today?

The Holocaust revealed horror stories about German merchants who sold lampshades made of human skin. But many times more Americans sell fur coats. And aren't fur coats an ugly reminder of those lampshades? Most people reacted with horror during the 1960s over news stories about a petty thief named Albert DeSalvo. In addition to committing a number of grisly murders, he claimed to have raped 2,000 women. Were the demeaning and unnatural aspects of the rapes not a more hideous but similar form of degradation as the American traditions of animal-punishing circuses and rodeos?

Ted Bundy stunned television viewers watching news coverage of his impending execution during the 1980s. His articulate manner sharply contrasted with his behavior as a serial killer. Were Bundy's random murders not a more advanced form of hunting?

The argument against animals' rights now sounds ridiculous upon reflection. Television commentator Patrick Buchanan suggested in 1990 that an animal bred to be eaten is better off than one who is not born and has no life at all. That is analogous to a ludicrous justification for child abuse on grounds that the victim is better off than one who was never born.

The philosopher Immanuel Kant contended that an alleged inability to reason precludes animals from having rights—which is analogous to denying civil liberties to a retarded person. A 1990 *Washingtonian* magazine article by animal-rights critic Katie McCabe begins with a photograph of a baby cuddling a cat. A caption reads: "Should researchers experiment on a cat so a baby can be saved from Sudden Infant Death Syndrome? Animal-rights activists say no." That caption irrationally suggests that torturing cats in the laboratory may be necessary to save that baby. And no mention is made of alternatives to using the cat, such as computer simulations and tissue or cell cultures.

A 1989 *Barron's* editorial by Robert M. Bleiberg attacked the animal-rights movement. The headline reads: "Animal Worship: It's Become a Clear and Present Danger to American Health and Welfare." An analogy can be drawn between that headline and a hypothetical one with a German dateline 50 years earlier that might have read: "Jewish Worship: It's Become a Clear and Present Danger to German Health and Welfare." In his 1960 book, *The Forest and the Sea,* Marston Bates states that "animals are unimportant because they have no souls." Who is Marston Bates, and does he have a soul?

Animals' rights have emerged through the same cycle by which minority groups of American have attained civil rights. It was a slow cycle—a cycle in which those in power collectively evolved from patterns of exploiting to ignoring, respecting, and finally defending the rights of others. Regarding animals, some individuals never advance beyond the beginning stage, exploiting, but their resistance is on a collision course with the more powerful and irrepressible animal-rights movement. They are a movable force set to collide with the irresistible momentum of an animal-rights movement that can no longer be contained.

The initial stage of exploiting animals involves the consuming or selling of products that require the pain and death of animals: consciously eating some animal's mother or wearing an animal's brother; using animals in medical or cosmetic research; manipulating animals in sports and entertainment; and hunting animals, regardless of the reason. There is only a fine line between exploiting animals and ignoring animals' rights.

Ignoring animals' rights means viewing what others eat, wear, and buy as none of your business; patronizing a company that animal-rights groups have targeted for boycott; making decisions on what to eat, wear, or buy without consideration of the impact on animals; and tolerating acts of animal neglect or abuse by another party.

Respecting animals' rights implies good intentions. But it is the motto of the People for the Ethical Treatment of Animals (PETA) that "good intentions are not enough." The philosophy of respecting animals' rights is demonstrated by acknowledging signs of emotion exhibited by an animal; recognizing when an animal acts upon reason rather than instinct; believing that an animal has a soul similar to humans'; recognizing the analogy between the plight of animals in the United States with that of human victims of genocidal wars or institutionalized slavery; accepting the right of an animal not to be subjected to pain; and adhering to a lifestyle that precludes eating, wearing or otherwise exploiting animals.

Defending animals' rights means respecting animals' rights and speaking out in support of those rights in the face of critics; drawing attention to what someone eats, wears, and buys or to whether that person hunts or supports vivisection; and making issue of any law that violates animals' rights. Criticizing someone who is in the process of purchasing meat or perhaps a leather product may overstep the bounds of commonly accepted etiquette; but remember, animals cannot speak for themselves.

Today's exploitation and annihilation carries something of the same perverted justifications that the Nazis used for human victims at Auschwitz, Buchenwald, Dachau, Mauthausen, Sachsenhausen and Treblinka. Medical experiments on designated "subhumans" were justified by German leaders as necessary to make advances for the benefit of their self-proclaimed superior Aryan race.

A young Jewish boy, whom we may call David, was forced to take part in one such experiment. You have seen how a vacuum cleaner sucks dirt out from a carpet. Imagine being placed in a room while all of its air is being sucked out by a giant vacuum cleaner. The pain he suffered drove him berserk. He pulled out his hair in an effort to relieve the pressure on his eardrums. He tore flesh from his face with his fingernails. He beat his head against the wall. And he screamed in agony until he was dead. Such experiments are described in more horrifying detail in William L. Shirer's *The Rise and Fall of the Third Reich* (Simon and Schuster, 1960).

What if a likeness of Lassie, the collie you know from television, were substituted for David in that experiment? The pain Lassie would feel would be the same as the boy's. Only the species would have changed.

Or, imagine further that a young girl, call her Sally, lives in your neighborhood. She becomes so sick that she immediately requires a very strong dose of a rare medicine to stay alive. Her father pounds frantically on your door. "We need to test Sally's medicine on Pantaloon!" he cries. Pantaloon is your companion poodle. Sally's father is a physician, who explains that time is of the essence. "I need to determine how big a dose would be lethal, but your dog—because she weighs so much less than Sally—may possibly not survive the test." Outside you spot a mangy dog of mixed breed, which seems to weigh approximately the same as Sally. An obviously retarded boy follows the dog, but it is obvious that the dog is a stray and not with the boy. Would you be tempted, if it were not a felony, to test the medicine on the retarded boy? Would you seize the stray dog? Or would you sacrifice Pantaloon? The only life you have a moral right to risk for this experiment is your own.

Suppose that you are at a party. The host serves a buffet containing filet mignon, which you would rarely have an opportunity to eat because of its cost. Sampling a small portion of the filet mignon is the moral equivalent of eating a full portion. A mere taste violates every principle behind the animal-rights movement. The temptation to violate a principle brings to mind the fable of a woman or man who is offered an outlandish sum of money to commit adultery. "For two million dollars, I suppose I would," the person concedes. "What about for two dollars?" "What do you think I am?" is the response. "We have already established that. Now it's just a question of haggling over the price."

Imagine that an extremely attractive, intelligent, and successful person expresses a romantic interest in you. Both of you are unattached. In casual conversation, the person recalls how long hours and job requirements to travel once made it necessary to have a companion animal destroyed. No mention is made of the probability that the person had taken the animal out of contention for a good home at her most marketable time. You could empathize with the person's dilemma and remorse. But would you feel the same if the person had abandoned, without support, a middle-aged spouse who had agreed to forego building credentials that would be needed to become marketable in a profession in order to raise that person's children?

A large hole has rendered your cruelty-free vinyl briefcase completely useless. You drive by a garage sale being laid out in an upscale neighborhood. There, ready for sale, is a genuine leather briefcase in perfect condition for only three dollars. The low price of that otherwise expensive leather product is misleading, because purchasing the briefcase would cost you your convictions,

Philosopher Peter Singer. (Photo by Scott D. Christopher, Courtesy of National Alliance for Animal Legislation)

principles, and ideals if you have evolved to the stage where you truly respect animals' rights.

Your supply of a cosmetic product that you regularly use is depleted. The product is advertised in a newspaper at half price by your local supermarket. As you clip the ad, you spot a story reporting how the manufacturer of that product is being boycotted by animal-rights' activists for experiments it has conducted in which animals were subjected to considerable pain and destroyed. You could stock up on the product because of its low price. If you respected animals' rights, you would purchase the more expensive alternative to the product. And if you had evolved to the extent that you defended animals' rights, you would write a letter to the general manager of the supermarket asking that the product not be stocked.

Imagine that you are in a position in which you consider yourself fortunate to receive the salary that your company pays. Suppose no other local company pays employees with similar job qualifications as much. You discover by accident that your company secretly conducts pain-tolerance experiments on animals by contract for another company. An exploiter of animals' rights would likely take measures to safeguard the evidence to keep it from coming to the attention of other employees who might not be as loyal as you. If you were one who ignored animals' rights, you would dismiss the evidence as irrelevant to your job. One who respects animals' rights, however, would immediately begin a search for an inevitably lower-paying job with another company. A defender of animals' rights would not only change jobs, but would turn the evidence over to an animal-rights organization.

8

A new family moves into your neighborhood. Their two poodles roam freely along the adjacent highway each morning, narrowly escaping death. Your spouse has twice brought this to the attention of your neighbor, but the dogs continue to run free. You mention the situation to a co-worker, who expresses a strong desire to provide the poodles with a safe home. You could offer an apology to the neighbor for your spouse's interference, mind your own business, report the situation to the local animal warden, or arrange to have your co-worker kidnap the dogs and save them.

Suppose that your daughter is given a mink stole by her male friend. You could advise your daughter to reject the gift and even to consider breaking the relationship.

You shake hands during a reception with a friend's husband, who introduces himself as a scientist involved with animal-based research. Your friend is a veterinarian. She expresses pride in her husband's work. He briefly describes the research as designed to determine the effect of coated aspirin on an empty stomach from hourly injections of the medicine to chimpanzees which have been starved for two days. A defender of animals' rights would very politely inform the experimenter that his use of chimpanzees is immoral and his veterinarian wife that her support of that research is hypocritical to her profession of helping animals—if such things could be said without creating a rude confrontation or embarrassing them, of course.

A business associate takes you to lunch with an important new client whom you are expected to host for the remainder of the week. The client asks if it would be possible to attend the circus that is in town. Before you can respond, the business associate hands you tickets to the circus. The client is excited. You recognize the circus as punishment and humiliation for the animals forced to be a part of it, but you do not want to risk losing your new client's account with what would undoubtedly be inferred as radical views on animals' rights. One who respects animals' rights would find a diplomatic way not to attend the circus. One who defends animals' rights would explain why.

Finally, you are canvassing your neighborhood to gain support for a congressional candidate in whom you have confidence. The opposing party is fielding a candidate you consider to be of poor character because of highly publicized financial dealings. Your canvassing appears to be evoking interest in the candidate you are backing. An influential neighbor answers the door wearing a fur coat. She conveys an intent to support your candidate, but asks you pointedly what you think of her coat. You could avoid the question with humor, perhaps remarking that it's not your size. At a minimum, one who respects animals' rights would not patronize the woman with an insincere compliment that could later serve to reinforce convictions to make subsequent purchases of fur. But why not simply tell her the truth?

Chapter 1

Defining Your Own Animal-Rights Philosophy

P sychologists David Krech, Richard S. Crutchfield, and Norman Livson twice reached into the pages of published works from the 1940s with the intention of demonstrating different points in their textbook *Elements of Psychology* (Alfred A. Knopf, 1969). From the Brown and Gilhousen text, *College Psychology* (Prentice-Hall, 1949), Krech and company borrowed an illustration of *failure to recognize* a figure that typically turns into *inability not to recognize* it after seeing the figure from a different perspective. They first displayed an illustration of the capitalized word "FLY" printed in white letters on a black background but without the black background above or below the three letters to completely define their shapes. Even after prolonged inspection, subjects typically experienced an inability to recognize the three-letter word. But after seeing the word printed in black letters on a white background, the same subjects were unable *not* to recognize the word when taking another look at the first illustration.

Certainly the lesson learned from Brown and Gilhousen applies to human recognition of animals' rights. And it could not be more evident than in another illustration borrowed from the 1940s that Krech, Crutchfield, and Livson intended to demonstrate another point. In 1940, a team of researchers named Maier, Glaser, and Klee published an article in *The Journal of Experimental Psychology* entitled "Studies of Abnormal Behavior in the Rat." A photograph of a captive rat appeared in the Krech text to demonstrate the effect of frustration coupled with punishment on problem-solving behavior in the rat. At first glance and perhaps even after prolonged inspection, a typical reader of that 1960s psychology text may be unable to recognize anything in the photograph that would distract from its intended representation of the authors' cited reference to the Maier team's research on "the effect of frustration coupled with punishment on problem-solving behavior in the rat." But, after realizing that the cited experiment was inflicting pain upon the rat, another glance at the photograph is likely to leave the reader unable to recognize anything in the photograph other than the obvious pain that the rat was enduring—just as readers at first could not identify the world "FLY," and then could see nothing but that.

You can use your reaction now as a basis for comparison to determine the extent to which, or if, your philosophy on animals' rights has evolved over the years. Was there a time when the inclusion of that study in a college textbook would have justified in your mind the contriving of a situation in which the helpless animal "bumped its nose and fell . . .[in] hundreds of successive trials"? Was there a time in which you would have had no opinion regarding the use of the rat in that experiment? Is it conceivable that you would support or at least not object to that study taking place now? Findings showed that the rat seemed "to have rigidly stereotyped behavior, experimentally induced through prolonged frustration." Could you imagine making a person bump his nose and fall hundreds of times in order to learn that? The pain from bumping its nose and the anguish over the frustration of repeatedly falling hurt the same in a rat as it would in a human.

In defining your animal-rights philosophy, it is helpful to look upon hypothetical decisions that may emanate from the philosophy in terms of moral equivalents to indisputable rights or wrongs. The decision to eat a piece of fried chicken does not carry the savage intent of an Idi Amin practicing cannibalism, but rather a desire to conform with one's peers; thus the two acts are not moral equivalents. On the other hand, within any crime-infested area are groups engaged in the most perverse acts imaginable, and within these groups are jaded participants who view what they do with nonchalance. In that context, it is a desire to conform with one's peers that drives someone to participate in a brutal assault—even one as horrendous as the attack, in 1989, which stained New York's Central Park with the loss of a woman jogger's dignity forever. Of course, that desire to conform was derived from a savage intent.

Defining your animal-rights philosophy inevitably begins with a guilt-driven conflict challenging your selection of animals' rights as a subject of concern over some other cause that would benefit humans; and it continues with guilt-ridden recognition of inconsistencies between that which you philosophically oppose and that which you do. The process may escalate into self-induced pressure to conform your various political and even religious beliefs with outspoken individuals who share a common philosophy on animals' rights.

Focusing attention on animals' rights implies no more of a slight on other causes than time or money spent for leisure activities; yet, the most frequent question posed to animal-rights activists concerns why they do not spend their efforts devoted to animals on homeless people or some other cause instead. Those who ask that question are typically not helping any cause at all.

The biggest burden imposed upon animal-rights activists is to avoid inconsistencies between what they preach and practice. The burden is such that it may become difficult for the person to recognize when indirect exploitation of animals is logically unavoidable and when it is a product of rationalization—rationalization that it is senseless to let the sacrifices of the animals be in vain. But just as it is logically unavoidable to use a road that was paved by slaves, it may also be unavoidable to use a drug that was tested on animals when there are no alternatives available. This does not suggest that testing of certain drugs on animals is necessary; it just acknowledges that sometimes no compassionate alternatives exist when industrial or governmental bodies do not bother to provide them.

The most perplexing aspect of addressing the animal-rights issue is to define a philosophy that is compatible with your other philosophies and beliefs while not necessarily being consistent. It is a misconception that animals' rights is a liberal issue. A President Edward M. Kennedy would very likely have sponsored as much or more vivisection as President Ronald Reagan did during

14

his two terms in office. The same could be said of Jesse Jackson and a host of other liberal candidates, if given a seat in the Oval Office. Animal-rights activists have shown no signs of a consensus on issues ranging from abortion and affirmative action to the United States' attack against Saddam Hussein. No person is more apt to favor an expanded recognition of animals' rights than anyone else. Despite inevitable attempts by proponents of other causes to recruit animal-rights advocates for their own purposes, there is no linkage between animals' rights and any other cause, because either side of almost every human issue can be rationalized as being consistent with the fairness and compassion inherent in the nonpartisan issue of animals' rights.

By now you probably have a preliminary notion regarding whether you are more apt to callously approve of the exploitation of animals, to apathetically ignore the issue of animals' rights, to simply respect the rights of animals, or to assertively defend animals' rights. That preliminary notion is likely to evolve toward a perceived philosophy that is supportive of defending animals' rights as you discover the truths about companion animals, vivisection, product testing on animals, hunting, fur, leather, meat, factory farming, and animals in sport and entertainment.

Regardless of your particular philosophy on animals' rights, and whether it does indeed evolve toward increased support, it is reasonable to assume that increased awareness of the issues will at least create a change in your perspective of those individuals who are actively involved with the movement. Every animal-rights activist is a spokesperson for the animals, and every animal needs a spokesperson insofar as the animals cannot speak for themselves.

That animals are personal property available for human use is the misconception that justified slavery in the United States. The most compelling reason for a human to dispel that misconception may have been best expressed, although unwittingly, by Richard Nixon. In his book *From the Arena* (Simon & Schuster, 1990), President Nixon recalled a lesson he learned after stepping down from power. It may offer special meaning as you struggle to develop your philosophy on animals' rights: "Unless a person has a reason to live for other than himself, he will die—first mentally, then emotionally, then physically." The former president undoubtedly found his reason to live by advancing human causes. But advancing human causes may not provide a human with the opportunity to self-lessly expand beyond himself, because humans benefit indirectly by helping other humans. Defending animals' rights presents a human with that reason to live for *other than himself.* And, most important, it is the right thing to do.

Your evolution toward a philosophy of defending animals' rights may become unsettling when you discover that inherent in your belief is an increasing level of support for civil disobedience. Perhaps, for personal reasons, that support may never reach the level at which you would participate, but you may become inclined to recognize that the animal-rights movement is not unlike every other cycle of positive social change—the type of change that historically has relied upon civil disobedience to force an issue into the glare of an inextinguishable spotlight.

In a book entitled *Concerning Dissent and Civil Disobedience* (New American Library, 1968), then-United States Supreme Court Justice Abe Fortas explained how nonviolent dissent can successfully achieve revolutionary goals within the law, institutions, and traditions of a democratic society. The book begins with a series of brief quotations from great minds. Among those quoted is philosopher Erich Fromm, who said, "Human history began with an act of disobedience—it is likely to end with an act of obedience."

Justice Fortas speculated that if he had lived in Nazi Germany, he hoped he "would have refused to wear an armband, to Heil Hitler, to submit to genocide. . . although Hitler's edicts were law." Perhaps in another half-century, a progressive Supreme Court justice will say that if he or she had lived during this era, the justice would have refused to hunt, eat meat, wear fur and leather, purchase products that were tested on animals, contribute money to charities that support vivisection, patronize circuses or rodeos, or submit to the genocide of animals.

But in limiting his definition of civil disobedience to "a person's refusal to obey a law which the person believes to be immoral or unconstitutional," Justice Fortas made clear that he would have disapproved of breaking one law to call attention to another. Under his definition, it is reasonable to assume that intentionally making noise to scare animals off to safety would constitute civil disobedience of hunter harassment laws, which specifically prohibit that; but it could also be assumed that trespassing or blocking traffic on a facility in order to protest animal experimentation taking place inside would not. That is because the laws prohibiting those acts, by themselves, would not be immoral. However, with that logic, Fortas would have had to "submit to genocide" if he had lived in Germany during the Holocaust, when six million Jews

17

were tortured to death in concentration camps—contrary to his speculation that he would have not. The Jewish martyrs were as powerless as animals in America today to disobey the laws that authorized their slaughter. So, if there were to have been civil disobedience in Germany during the Holocaust, the burden would have fallen upon German citizens to focus world attention on the situation by breaking other laws—perhaps those prohibiting disorderly conduct—by blocking the railroad tracks transporting Jews to death camps. But there was none.

The void of civil disobedience in the United States protesting the Holocaust was best captured by the late Rabbi Meir Kahane, almost a quarter of a century before his 1990 assassination, in excerpts from his book *Never Again* (Nash Publications, 1971). In reflecting back on what he termed a deafening silence "obscenely empty of any vigorous sacrifice" on the part of American Jewish leaders, Rabbi Kahane noted that "those who later went to jail in Selma for the cause of civil rights did not even consider the possibility of chaining themselves to the White House gates in 1939 to call attention to the plight of the 930 passengers of the ill-fated ship, the *St. Louis,* who, themselves, symbolized millions of others on the brink of slaughter."

The rabbi several times made mention of the documented fact that President Franklin Delano Roosevelt denied the 930 Jewish refugees from Hitler entrance into the United States because of a quota system he had been maintaining. Rabbi Kahane suggested that millions of lives would have been spared had pressure been brought upon Roosevelt to allow entry of Jewish refugees into the United States and to bomb German rail lines used to transport Jews to the death camps—the bridges over which the rail lines ran—as well as the death camp areas, to put them out of commission. Civil disobedience could have provided that pressure. But there was none. To those who hold a philosophy supportive of defending animals' rights, Roosevelt's resolve to do nothing may be analogous to contemporary American presidents who react with similar indifference while animals are being slaughtered by the millions in the United States.

*E*ven the most militant animal-rights activist would likely accept the concept of civil disobedience as being nonviolent dissent, meaning that no people or animals should ever be hurt in the process. But the use of civil disobedience as a means of defending animals' rights presents an issue that has long divided the movement. A philosophy supportive of defending animals' rights is not necessarily one that would approve of civil disobedience, despite the fact that a 1985 sit-in at the National Institute of Health over PETA videotapes of head injuries inflicted on primates at the University of Pennsylvania ended with Secretary of Health and Human Services Margaret M. Heckler pulling the funds from the government-sponsored laboratory—which then stopped that gruesome torture. No person should ever encourage another to break the law.

There is a widely held misconception that animal-rights activists who participate in sit-ins such as the afore-mentioned one, or in any type of civil disobedience, are radicals. Generally speaking, they are not. They are, however, liberals with respect to the animal-rights issue because of their demonstrated desire to reform, regardless

CELEBRITIES JOIN THE BATTLE

A banner appealing for the release of monkeys subjected to vivisection that resulted in the first conviction of an experimentor for animal cruelty. (L. to R.: Jane Wiedlin of the Go-Gos; Cassandra Peterson, a.k.a. Elvira; Buddy Silverman, the author of this book; Grace Slick, formerly of the Jefferson Airplane and Starship, with such classic hits as "White Rabbit" and "Miracles"; cartoonist Berke Breathed ("Bloom County" and "Outland"); actress Peggy McKay ("The Days of Our Lives"); Cleveland Amory, President of the Fund for Animals; actress Gretchen Wyler ("Bye-Bye Birdie").
(Photo by Scott D. Christopher, courtesy of the National Alliance for Animal Legislation)

of whether they hold conservative positions on other social or economic issues. Many radicals participate in civil disobedience for animals' rights, but not many who participate in civil disobedience for animals' rights are radicals. Saul D. Alinsky best captured the difference between a liberal and radical in his book *Reveille for Radicals* (Vintage Books, 1969): "Liberals protest; radicals rebel. Liberals become indignant; radicals become fighting mad and go into action. . . . Liberals frequently achieve high places of respectability, ranging from Supreme Court to Congress; the names of radicals are rarely inscribed in marble." Alinsky's depiction of liberals as frequently achieving high places of respectability is largely true about animal-rights activists; and many of those in high places participate in civil disobedience.

The emergence of celebrities into the animal-rights movement has made defending animals' rights the right thing to do, both morally and socially. As the celebrities transfer their attractive images to activists who are erroneously perceived as being representative of a fringe element, the movement has drifted into the mainstream. Ironically, most animal-rights activists do come from society's mainstream; and the desirable traits transferred from celebrities are not uncharacteristic in any segment of the movement. Just as the more attractive actors and actresses have catapulted ordinary situation comedies to the top of television ratings, the growing recognition that attractive and successful people support animals' rights has begun to project the movement as a prestigious affiliation. As it drifts into the mainstream, the animal-rights movement is becoming permanently anchored as an emotional issue that may compel almost every literate person at some point to be conscious—if not considerate—of how their lifestyles affect animals.

Even with the animal-rights movement firmly entrenched in the mainstream of society, irrepressible detractors will find a way to distort the moderate opinions of animal-rights activists into extremist positions. Such was the case in 1986 when one of the most prominent leaders of the animal-rights movement remarked on network television that there was no difference in the feeling of pain in a rat, a pig, a dog, or a boy. For years, that statement would be brought up as alleged evidence of irrational thinking, after it had been distorted in meaning to suggest that there is no difference in intellect between rats, pigs, dogs, or little boys. In 1990, one of the most prominent celebrities in Hollywood made a statement to the effect that no living being should ever have to jeopardize himself to test drugs on any disease, but that volunteered participation in such experiments by convicted killers would be less objectional than the current use of animals "because I can't bear anything innocent being used." But the celebrity's statement made headlines with out-of-context quotes favoring Nazi-like torture of prisoners when, in fact, that had not been suggested at all.

Whenever an animal-rights activist compares the traditional human attitude toward animals as allegedly being "a lower form of life" with racism, detractors are quick to claim that the intent is to compare the biological differences between humans and animals with genetic differences that are alleged to exist between white Americans and Afro-Americans, Asians, and other victims of racism.

Comparing the techniques used to kill Jewish people and others by German Schutzstaffel (SS) officers with the mass slaughter of dogs and cats draws charges of diminishing the magnitude of the Holocaust. The prejudice that resulted in more than six million innocent victims of Nazi genocide was obviously immeasurably worse than the daily slaughter of dogs and cats that takes place in animal shelters throughout the United States today, because the innocent victims' horrible fate was inflicted upon them with malice. Homeless dogs and cats are victims only of human selfishness, because animals are not self-reliant. Nor are most animals in laboratories victims of malice; they are victims of human greed and ignorance. The genocide during the Holocaust is without question the worst tragedy that has ever happened to mankind. But the collective pain and loss of dignity that Jews and others suffered are analogous to what animals tolerate today.

The argument against a philosophy supportive of defending animals' rights rests upon acceptance of obvious errors in logic that range from statements such as "There is a consensus in the medical community that vivisection is vital to human health, so animals must continue to be sacrificed for the advancement of science" to assertions that "Medical researchers under federal government grants take every precaution to make their animal subjects as comfortable as possible."

The first statement—about a consensus in the medical community—is obviously fallacious because it ignores the many alternatives to animal research that make it un-necessary; it makes no mention of the huge government grants and opportunities for publication (advancing animal researchers' careers) that vivisection brings; and it denies the overriding fact that the use of animals as subjects in research is basically immoral. The statement about animal

23

researchers taking every precaution to make their subjects as comfortable as possible is obviously a classic example of self-contradiction. The most frequent error in logic operates under the assumption that if one event precedes another, the first event must cause the second. That fallacy is applied when attributing unrelated increases in longevity or decreases in outbreaks of disease to vivisection; and even when attempting to find a scapegoat for failures in medical science. For example, philosopher Peter Singer propelled the animal-rights movement to new heights with his book *Animal Liberation* (Avon, 1977), a few years before the outbreak of the AIDS epidemic. Had vivisection been curtailed at that time, the subsequent AIDS epidemic may well have been cited as a direct result.

Only in German concentration camps did human beings ever have to make arbitrary choices regarding which of their loved ones they preferred to save. Yet, defenders of animals' rights are frequently tested with the question "Who would you save, between your animal companion and a human, if you could save only one?" The obvious answer is that you always save the one you love. In a speech after the historic June 10, 1990, March for the Animals in Washington, D.C., prominent cartoonist Berke Breathed satirized this line of thinking by facetiously asking whether one would save the life of an animal over murderer Charles Manson.

The logic behind a philosophy supportive of defending animals' rights is most evident when humans are viewed in traditional animal roles. There is nothing funny about eating chicken. But a joke handed down over many generations uses humor to demonstrate that eating chicken is barbaric. The joke has a butcher reassuring a persistent customer that his chickens are fresh. With a drumstick in each hand, the customer brings the chicken close and inhales deeply. "It doesn't smell fresh," the customer complains. After a deliberate pause, the butcher looks deeply into the customer's eyes and responds, "Could you pass that test?"

During the telecast of a football game between the Washington Redskins and Dallas Cowboys in 1990 on Thanksgiving Day, a sportscaster made reference to the enormous size of an offensive lineman and quipped, "How would you like to be the turkey and have him come home to you tonight?" Again, the intended humor is created by an element of truth. Putting yourself in place of the turkey and visualizing some giant about to eat you evokes a concept of something terribly wrong.

Defending animals' rights may put you in direct conflict with people who actually like animals, despite their thoughtless and unfortunate actions that harm them. It may not occur to many beneficiaries of animal-based trades that they thrive on animal consumption or, in other words, on animal destruction. It is with these people that sharing a philosophy supportive of defending animals' rights may exert a positive effect. One who ignorantly contributes to the exploitation of animals does not have to be ignorant and may, in fact, be a gentle person. But it is difficult to distinguish between a gentle person and one not so gentle who is simply soft-spoken. For every gentle person abusing animals out of ignorance, there is one equally as soft-spoken who does it for fun. It is with these people that actions speak louder than words.

Philosopher Thomas Hobbes held that individuals are not morally responsible for immoral acts that they perform for their government. That line of reasoning enables many vivisectors and other animal abusers to rationalize their innocence by detaching themselves from what they do. Under that line of reasoning, Hobbes would have exonerated Nazi Adolf Eichmann—a man who was just doing his job, and doing it with a smile.

The pursuit and capture of Eichmann is covered in *The House on Garibaldi Street* (Viking, 1975) by Isser Harel, former Chief of the Israeli Secret Service. In many ways, Eichmann was much like the soft-spoken people who abuse animals for fun. Several sources, including a movie based upon Harel's book, have quoted Eichmann as having allegedly said in his soft voice that he would go to his grave smiling with the knowledge that he had contributed so much toward the killing of six million Jews; and he did. This is how Harel described Eichmann: "I didn't know that he was capable of ordering the slaughter of babies—and depicting himself as a disciplined soldier; of directing outrages on women—and priding himself on his loyalty to an oath." Memories of Adolf Eichmann's unsuccessful defense for Nazi war crimes were evoked when—according to PETA records—a laboratory assistant, who had direct responsibility for care of the Silver Spring Monkeys, had criminal charges dropped at the outset when a judge ruled that the assistant had only followed orders.

The most difficult part of defending animals' rights is determining whether the person whose abuse of animals requires your intervention has the smile of a gentle person or that of an Adolf Eichmann. While the damaging impact that their particular roles exert does not occur to many beneficiaries of animal abuse, someone with an Adolf

Eichmann smile may lurk in the kitchen of a fine res-
taurant that serves meat, in a fitting room of an elite store
that sells leather and fur, in the front-row seat of a rodeo
or circus that exploits animals, in the executive offices of
a company that tests its products on animals, and within
the confines of a laboratory that conducts hideous perversions on animals under the name of science. When
approached by animal-rights activists for wearing fur, one
very prominent personality—known for having a particularly warm smile—said, "They're nasty, dirty little
animals who deserve to die." It is doubtful whether rational
discussion would have saved the life of a single Jew during
the Holocaust, if the person being addressed was Adolf
Eichmann.

*A*lthough defending animals' rights is the right thing to
do, it may not always be the wisest thing, depending
upon the circumstances. Speaking out in support of
animals' rights is the right thing to do, but it is a waste of
time if the critics are closed-minded. Your termination of
a friendship because of what the other person eats, wears,
or buys may result in your having an unnecessarily lonely
existence without accomplishing anything. Confronting
acquaintances on what they are eating or wearing could
be hazardous to your career, especially if one of those
acquaintances happens to be your boss. Taking this a step
further, and confronting total strangers, could result in
your being physically assaulted without altering anything
other than your appearance. Making issue of a law that
violates animals' rights could result in your being arrested
if you break the law in the process. And criticizing animal

abuse by a company or entertainer could result in your being sued.

Ironically, the answer to the question regarding when to assertively extend oneself in defense of animals' rights resembles the response to the same question posed at the end of a satirical radio commercial in the Washington, D.C., area during the 1980s that promoted ice cream—a product that is typically derived through "factory farming." In the commercial, the voice of a woman laments having eaten an entire box, and a man is heard doing the same for having made a fool of himself by eating portions intended for children. But both the woman and the man reluctantly answer, "Yeah!" when asked, "Was it worth it?" That is the question one should anticipate before acting upon a philosophy to defend animals' rights. If situations are carefully selected, seldom will the answer be "No."

Just as the Watergate scandal eventually boiled down to the questions of what President Nixon knew and when he knew it, the animal-rights issue can be reduced to the simple questions of whether a species feels pain and if it can anticipate it. If the answers are "Yes," those species are proprietors of the same rights as humans to preserve their particular niche in the environment. The movement away from belief in a hierarchy of species is most succinctly expressed in the May 23, 1988, issue of *Newsweek,* in which reference was made to Australian philosopher Peter Singer, having in 1975 "coined the term 'speciesism,' by analogy to 'racism,' to describe mankind's traditional attitude toward so-called lower animals"; and to the observation from Dr. Neil Barnard, Chair of the Physicians Committee for Responsible Medicine, that both humans and animals have a "niche." In the words of Dr. Barnard:

"Dogs have more sensitive hearing and sense of smell. We have a more developed problem-solving ability. Every species has its own capability that allows us to exist."

Carrying Dr. Barnard's point a step further, it is apparent that virtually every species has traits that give it abilities vastly superior to those of humans. In addition to dogs' superior abilities to hear and smell, cats can see and climb better. The most timid lion could make mincemeat of the World Heavyweight Boxing Champion. And even the most courageous human, if of sound mind, would not attempt to fly like a bird. Dolphins, elephants, and whales have larger brains than humans and probably more compassion, in view of how, as professor Tom Regan so graphically put it in the *Newsweek* article, "we chop them up in laboratories, we fricassee them on the skillet." In defining your own animal-rights philosophy, the litmus test of compatibility is not how you want to feel about animals but how you want animals to feel about you.

"When is it ethical to subject unwilling individuals to painful procedures and death? Never. And it is only from a solid ethical foundation that productive science can grow."
—Neal D. Barnard, M.D., Chair, Physicians Committee for Responsible Medicine

Portrait of Lady Pompie, Cappuccino, and the author.

Chapter 2

Companion Animals

A companion animal is a lifetime partner of a different species who establishes a relationship with a human as a domesticated ambassador for animals' rights. "Companion animal" is a term of respect that takes into account the animal's individual needs and feelings. It implies a loving relationship, whereas the term "pet" implies ownership.

Animals considered pets can, in the wrong hands, become playthings for amusement or abuse. Violations of pets' rights come at the discretion of the individual "owner." Pets have no security, certainly no guarantee of the way in which they will be treated. Owners can keep pets in substandard or unsafe conditions or leave them homeless at any stage of their life—to face premature death at a shelter, on the streets, or in a research laboratory.

Everyday contact with companion animals should enable most humans to realize the terror that would compound their companions' physical suffering if they were as unfortunate as other animals to be placed in a laboratory for torture by needless experimentation or in a slaughterhouse to be ground into meat; but it does not. Most humans do not realize what animals endure.

Companion animals exhibit patterns of thought, action,

Buddy and Pompo Silverman. Many companies would love to have dogs like these, so that they could pour products like laundry detergent down their throats to protect themselves against potential consumer complaints.

Cappuccino Silverman welcomes Lady Pompie. Innocent animals like these are needlessly cut apart in medical schools, frequently without anesthesia.

32

and emotion that enable humans to recognize them as having souls comparable to humans' and rights equal to humans'. Unfortunately, most people do not. Most animals considered companion animals by "owners" are really pets.

My personal experiences with animal emotion have come in the form of pride exhibited by my companion dogs. As a young collie, my partner Lady Pompie marked her achievements by a wagging tail and bobbing head in utter excitement over catching a tennis ball or knotted rag. During her youth, she would show great intensity over running a correct pass route and bitter disappointment over a pass that fell incomplete. Her grand-uncle, Buddy, showed both modesty and a sensitive sense of decorum by refusing to go to the bathroom in front of anyone. When a skin rash required the white coat to be shaved from my earliest companion, Stroupie, being the proud spitz that he was, he bowed his head in humiliation until the hair grew back. It should be apparent from a wide variety of animal behavior that animals are conscious of more than what most people generally give them credit for.

After Pompo, my boyhood poodle companion, once uncharacteristically snapped at me, he immediately smothered me with affection to demonstrate that he was sorry. Since he had never even been admonished by any-one in his life, this touching affection was inspired solely through his own nature as distinct from conditioned fear or obedience. Further evidence of an animal's acting upon thought and emotion was seen by my father, at age 83, in a toy white poodle named Cappuccino, who would stare patiently at my father and wait for him to awaken each morning before asking to be let out. All of this suggests that the reasons traditionally given for believing that humans have souls are true of animals as well. Animals act on the basis of reason, not simply instinct.

You can see intelligence in your companion animal when he or she conveys signs of displeasure as you reach for his or her toothbrush, embarrassment after he or she makes a rare mistake on the carpet, and excitement as you pick up his or her walking leash. In the cover story of the May 23, 1988, *Newsweek* issue, author Geoffrey Cowley supports his theme of animals' having more intelligence than humans believe with authoritative opinions that dogs, in particular, have an uncanny ability to read someone's intentions—with the example of a guide dog first looking to see if his blind companion *wants* a dropped item back before picking it up. This suggests that an animal has the capacity to anticipate anguish in the same way as a human.

Those accustomed to treating their companion animals with care and consideration may find it difficult to imagine viewing animals they eat or wear in the same way—yet those animals feel pain in the same way. An animal can anticipate the horror of pain exactly the way a human would, if placed in a laboratory to be tortured or in a slaughterhouse to be ground into meat—as perverse as that sounds. The casual way in which some people inflict pain on animals is no different from the nonchalance many would exhibit if given the same risk-free opportunity to inflict pain on humans. Photographs from laboratories, of dead dogs piled on top of dead cats, are reminiscent of the Word War II photos displaying piles of dead Jews that were presented as evidence to convict German war criminals during the Nuremberg Trials.

As incredible as it may seem, the tragic impact of animal destruction in labs, farms, slaughterhouses and elsewhere is not the most compelling problem for domesticated animals. It is overpopulation. Projections in PETA literature hold that some 17 million healthy dogs and cats are put to death in animal shelters every year; and the actual number steadily increases at a gruesome pace because of birth rates that substantially exceed their natural death rates.

Most people readily admit that they value the lives of their particular loved ones over the lives of those they have not met and particularly those they do not like, except in cases where their loved one is a companion animal and the other party is a human being. One adult student at a university rejected the suggestion by his professor that he valued the life of his companion animal over the lives of his classmates in that room until he was reminded that he had spent in excess of a thousand dollars on an orthopedic operation for his companion animal and was invited to do the same for any human outside his immediate family; the student conceded the point. I was that professor.

What to do each year with the 17 million potential companion animals who are homeless is a question that divides many in the animal-rights movement. The majority of published works on this issue reluctantly favor euthanasia. PETA literature on the subject recommends death by injection for the following reasons: "Companion animals cannot survive on the streets. If they don't starve, freeze, get hit by a car, or die of disease, they may be tormented and possibly killed by bored juveniles or picked up by a dealer who obtains animals to sell to laboratories."

Many who cannot bring themselves to accept that option salvage as many lives as they can in no-kill shelters such as Friends of Homeless Animals (also known as Friends of the Animal Shelter) in northern Virginia. A flyer of that organization described some of the since-adopted inhabitants:

> Josh loves to roll on his back and have his tummy rubbed. . . General [was] voted "Most Attractive" by his dog friends. . . Blackie needs a special home. Despite his fading eyesight, he's still champ at playing ball. . . . Muffin's tail has never stopped wagging despite being passed over for adoption year after year. . . . Walker loves to curl up on your lap and give kisses.

One success story for Friends of Homeless Animals appeared in the October 21, 1990, issue of the *Washington Post*, under the headline "The Dog Nobody Wanted," in a story by Joseph Cerquone about a homeless canine ignored for five years, who finally found a home. This is the story of Opie:

> Desperate to place Opie, Friends of Homeless Animals finally dubbed him "Pet of the Week" and featured his picture in a newspaper ad that I happened to notice. Opie looked okay in the ad, but. . . an old scar marred the top of his head. Part of his left ear was gone. . . I was coaxed by Friends to "give the ol' boy a chance." I am glad I listened to them. Today, Opie is very wanted—by me, by my family, by neighborhood kids.

36

Retired Judge Anne P. Lewis, President of Friends of Homeless Animals, said this about her no-kill shelter: "We limit the number of animals we take in so that they can be kept comfortable and contented. Our animals have a lot of human companionship and individual attention. If they cannot be kept this way, we do not take them in." (Many activists question the quality of life in no-kill shelters.)

Another potential problem at no-kill shelters is the threat of violence from disturbed people who need an outlet for their repressed hostility. Thus, the goodness of those who make considerable sacrifices to run these shelters can become a catalyst for human character disorders, creating situations in which the animals become targets for savage attacks. Such was the case that was reported by Laurie DeLater in the September 30, 1990, issue of the *Cleveland Plain Dealer* under the headline "Three Dogs of Animal Activist Are Killed." Activist Anita Zavodny had rescued a collie, an airedale, and a German shepherd from death at an animal shelter only to find them brutally murdered and a man she quoted as saying, "Now all your dogs are dead."

Individuals can avoid contributing to the overpopulation problem by having their companion animals submit to spaying or neutering operations if there is any chance that the animals will ever be unsupervised with animals of the opposite sex, or by bringing homeless animals into their families as an alternative to purchasing commercially bred animals. When homeless animals are adopted to become companion animals, potential revenue is taken from the hands of those commercial breeders who would stop adding to the animal population if there were no profit in store for them.

If the one adopting the animal is not concerned about the animal's well-being, adoption can be the beginning of greater problems for the animal. Some adopters consider their adopted animals beholden to them. The quid pro quo is translated into the adopter's feeling free to treat them in any way—even if that means abuse. That is when an animal needs a compassionate human most.

Witnessing an hour-long attack on a dog, Jim Molloy of Lowell, Massachusetts, had the presence of mind to take thirty snapshots that were used in court to send the assailant to jail for six months; one of the photos appeared in the April 30, 1990, issue of *People* magazine. The photo shows the convicted assailant stomping a helpless German shepherd mix, who is lying on his side and crying out for help. Yet the assailant's mother is quoted as saying that her convicted son "never beat that dog," and the family had already begun legal proceedings to regain custody of it. There is no indication that Jim Molloy had ever given prolonged consideration to the issue of animals' rights. But when he saw a defenseless animal being abused, he instinctively knew that defending animals' rights is the right thing to do.

In 1989, the *Washington Post* reported how similar instincts compelled Trans World Airlines ramp worker David Perriello to run waist-high into the freezing Potomac River at National Airport—risking his own life—to rescue a Shetland sheep dog which had escaped from a travel kennel on an airplane. "I just went in and broke through the ice until I got to him," Mr. Perriello was quoted as saying. It was Perriello's natural instinct to save the struggling animal, as reported in the *Post* article by Nell Henderson: "I saw him start to go under. I knew I had to act fast."

Ironically, the companion animals most in need of human defense are those thought to be most capable of defending themselves. The January 22, 1990, *USA Today* debate page presented as many people in favor of outlawing pit bulls as not. Outlawing pit bulls, of course, means killing them. An authoritative opposing voice was that of Dr. Neil Wolff, Associate of Veterinarians for Animal Rights, who was quoted as saying: "We should be concerned not with the dogs as a breed, but with the people who train them to violence."

Also in 1990, Retha Hill and Gabriel Escobar reported in the *Washington Post* that an off-duty Montgomery County police officer shot and killed a rottweiler after she had bitten the officer's wrist as he tried to confine her. The dead rottweiler was one of two who roamed on a playground. According to the *Post* article, "a few students... petted the dogs, who did not appear menacing, teacher Paul Graham said." No charges were ever brought against that police officer.

A much more touching companion animal story appeared in *USA Today* during the mid-1980s. It was about animal-rights activist Cole McFarland, who lost a leg leaping in front of a train to push his Irish setter companion off the tracks. The newspaper quoted Mr. McFarland as saying: "It's a question of values. Given the alternative of being the kind of person who would have two legs and have his dog crushed by a train or lose a leg and have my dog, I would rather be the latter. There are no regrets at all."

In the April 11, 1988, issue of the *Washington Post,* a white spitz named Teddy was reported to have inherited a trust fund and free roam of his deceased companion's house in Silver Spring, Maryland, until he had lived out his years in it. Although few companion animals are remembered by their human companions in such a dramatic way, there are always those who treat their beloved animals with the same respect that is traditionally reserved for blood relatives. Although this attitude is not a prerequisite for being an effective defender of animals' rights, this ability to perceive an animal as a true family member is one indication that you have chosen to honor the relationship between you and your companion animal beyond the 'speciesism' that predominates popular belief. It almost certainly demonstrates a fundamentally positive position towards animal protection and an even-handed recognition of the real contribution that animals make in the lives of their human companions.

*T*he love between many millions of Americans and their companion animals is everlasting, and nowhere is this more evident than in Silver Spring's Aspin Hill Memorial Park—formerly known as Aspin Hill Pet Cemetery, until its acquisition by PETA in 1988. Each of the remembrance markers, some dating as far back as the 1920s, for the nearly 50,000 animals buried there seems to say "I love you" in a different way.

That is why the Battle of Aspin Hill is one of the most inspiring love stories of all time. It was a story in which people from all walks of life banded together for two years in defense of the graves holding the remains of their departed companion animals. These were people who, for the most part, had never engaged in activism, but, when put to the test, recognized that defending animals' rights is indeed the right thing to do. It was a story in which several hundred plot holders, many of them elderly, waged an improbable battle against a prominent developer who

Lady Pompie Silverman watches over the grave of her grand-uncle
Buddy and namesake Pompo at Aspin Hill. (Photo by author)

wanted to build office condominiums on the grounds and
won as stunning a victory for the dignity of companion
animals as has ever been recorded. At the time, there were
no covenants on the land safeguarding its use as a burial
place for companion animals and no written contracts
guaranteeing the perpetual care that had been promised,
although videotape from a television show did record the
cemetery directory stating that perpetual care was included
in the cost of burial there.

The developer's plans for building on the cemetery's
sacred grounds appeared, to most observers, to be destined
for approval. But enormous political pressure from the plot
holders culminated in an upset victory, when the Montgomery County Council voted to deny the developer's bid.
The cemetery was eventually sold to a philanthropist and
donated to PETA with written assurances for perpetual

care, irrevocable covenants protecting the grave sites, and provisions for plot holders—this author included, whose heart is buried at Aspin Hill—to have burials in additional sites. The land surrounding the graves, on which the office condominiums would have been built, became a sanctuary instead for sheep, pigs, rabbits, chickens, and chinchillas to roam under PETA care as ambassadors for vegetarian, fur-free, and cruelty-free living. PETA National Director Ingrid Newkirk greeted plot holders with a letter that stated:

> We want Aspin Hill to be a true and everlasting memorial to those innocent, remarkable beings— our animals friends and companions—who have brought such joy and happiness into our lives before being laid to rest here. Aspin Hill is a tribute to the bond of perpetual love between them and those whose lives they touched. . . . The love and compassion these animals knew is what PETA wants for all animals: the hen in the factory farm, unable to stretch her wings; the monkey caged in the laboratory; the veal calf chained in his crate. . .

The significance of the name change from Aspin Hill Pet Cemetery to Aspin Hill Memorial Park reflects not only its expanded representation as a sanctuary and animal-rights education center, but the sentiment of many activists within the animal-rights movement. They view the word "pet" as a "speciesist" slur. It implies ownership over, or a subordinate role in the relationship for, the animal.

The term "speciesism" was coined by Peter Singer when he helped launch the animal-rights movement with his book *Animal Liberation.* " 'Speciesism,' " he wrote, "by analogy with racism, must also be condemned. Species-ism . . . is a prejudice or attitude of bias toward the interests of members of one's own species and against those of members of other species."

Taking a non-speciesist stance toward your companion animal is a first step toward defending animals' rights. That could mean a monumental demonstration of respect, such as naming a child after your companion animal or even adding the name to your own, as I did in 1975 and again in 1990 to perpetually enunciate the co-equality in our non-speciesist relationships; or it could mean a less drastic symbolic gesture, such as tasting the food you most fre-quently feed your companion animals or sleeping where your companion animal ordinarily sleeps.

This is not to suggest that you should change your name to Rover or Puff, eat disgusting dog or cat food, and sleep in the garage or even outside. I am merely suggesting that if you give your companion animal a dignified name, you will be less likely to discriminate with speciesism; and that domestic animals should never be given disgusting food or an uncomfortable place to sleep. Proper food and accommodations will improve their self-esteem; and those are the most important things you can do for a companion animal. The most important consideration for your companion animal is not how it feels about you, but how it feels about itself.

The Companion Animal Right-Thing-to-Do Review

True or False

____ 1. Finding a permanent and safe home yourself for a stray animal is better than placing the animal in a shelter, where his or her presence would create added competition to those already there and he or she would have only a limited stay before facing death.

____ 2. Depriving your companion animal of the opportunity to have sexual relations with members of his or her species is punishment too cruel to inflict upon humans; therefore, it is a speciesist act and the wrong thing to do.

____ 3. Giving your companion animal a name fit for a human is a logical first step in treating the animal with respect.

____ 4. The best thing to do when observing blatant animal abuse is to report the matter to authorities.

44

___F___ 5. The right thing to do in the spirit of animals' rights is to let fleas roam free on your companion animal.

___T___ 6. If your companion animal makes a mess on the carpet, it would only be acceptable to put the animal's nose in it if you put your nose in it first.

___F___ 7. The best thing to do for companion animals is to leave them alone and let them create their own type of animal entertainment.

___F___ 8. Because animals have more delicate stomachs than humans, the best thing to do when they get sick is to give them a non-aspirin pain reliever like Tylenol.

___F___ 9. The best thing to do with your companion animal when visitors drop by is to isolate the animal away from your company.

___T___ 10. The right thing to do with your companion animal to avoid being a speciesist is to provide the animal with accommodations equivalent to those provided to human members of the household.

Answers to the True or False Questions

1. The first statement is true.

2. The second statement is false.
    Concerns for the overpopulation of domesticated animals must override any freedom to reproduce. Unfortunately, there is not yet humane, easily accessible birth control for animals.

3. The third statement is true.

4. The fourth statement is false.
    While reporting blatant animal abuse is an important thing to do, the best thing would be to try to stop it as it is happening.

5. The fifth statement is false.
    Fleas are predators whose presence on your companion animal is harmful. Just as you would protect your child from bed bugs and lice, protect your companion animal from fleas.

6. The sixth statement is true.
    When my partner Lady Pompie was a puppy, we took a course in dog obedience in Arlington, Virginia. An instructor demonstrated how to get her attention by lifting up her leash so that she could momentarily experience the pain of being hanged. The fact that I allowed that to happen is something I will have to live with for the rest of my life. The same instructor also advised me to stick my companion's nose in her urine whenever she made a mess in the house. That is something I never did.

46

As the musical group Three Dog Night so aptly put it: "How can people be so cruel?"

Dana Spring, co-founder of Disabled and Incurably Ill for Alternatives to Animal Research, protests for animals' rights.
(Photo courtesy of Dana Spring)

7. The seventh statement is false.
   Domesticated animals need social contact with humans for their psychological well-being.

8. The eighth statement is false.
   In fact, Tylenol can kill animals. One of the reasons why vivisection is so wrong is because—in addition to immorally subjecting innocent animals to torture—the biological makeup of animals is not the same as that of humans. Lessons learned from testing human medication on animals may have no value whatsoever. Never administer medication designed for humans to animals, and never administer medicine designed for one species of animal to another. Medicine prescribed for a dog may kill a cat with the same ailment.

9. The ninth statement is true.

10. The tenth statement is true.

Chapter 3

The Use of Animals in Medical Experiments

Vivisection means cutting into a live animal for money or scientific curiosity. It is tantamount to raising a morbid question and receiving an outlandish sum of money to obtain the answer, the money coming generally from the federal government and the answer coming at the expense of what could be someone's companion animal—an animal caged with its feces and subjected to the most hideous perversions imaginable in order to reach a conclusion so predictable that it would have occurred to anyone without even conducting the study; or a conclusion that is so irrelevant that there would be no benefit in knowing it.

What makes matters worse is the fact that the answer to these morbid questions could have been obtained by not even involving the animal in the experiment, but through the use of advances in technology.

The number of animals in laboratories in the United States at any given time ranges high into the millions—20 million, 50 million, or perhaps even 100 million—depending upon the source and definition of a laboratory animal. It was the torture of seventeen monkeys in Silver Spring, Maryland, that put the spotlight on vivisection in 1981. Because of a daring undercover investigation conducted by Alex Pacheco, then a college student and co-founder, along with Ingrid Newkirk, of People for the Ethical Treatment of Animals, the seventeen monkeys would become known forever as the Silver Spring Monkeys and go on to symbolically represent the plight of laboratory animals everywhere.

PETA Chairperson Alex Pacheco appears with actress Rue McClanahan and singer Lene Lovich. (Photo courtesy of PETA)

By gaining entrance to the laboratory as a trusted volunteer, Pacheco collected enough evidence to result in the first conviction of a vivisector in the United States for animal cruelty. The conviction was later overturned on appeal that federally funded experimenters do not have to obey state anti-cruelty laws. When it was reported in 1990 that seven surviving Silver Spring Monkeys faced more laboratory torture, more than 46,000 readers responded with requested letters to PETA for First Lady Barbara Bush.

Earlier that year, PETA had released photographs of the Silver Spring Monkeys that were too gruesome for inclusion in this book. The suggested captions understated graphical illustrations of incomprehensible animal abuse.

One caption for a photograph stated that "physical and mental anguish...caused them to self-mutilate out of stress and fear." Another explained how the "experiments involved severing the nerves in the monkeys' spines, arms, and legs; and then tormenting the animals to force them to use their crippled limbs." The look on the faces of the monkeys shown in these photographs was even more heart-wrenching than the photographs of the monkeys with the self-mutilated arm. Another photograph showed a monkey spread-eagled in bondage. The caption stated that "Alex Pacheco observed crudely restrained primates subjected to 'acute noxious stimuli': burned with cigarette lighters and pinched with surgical pliers." The caption for yet another ghastly photograph explained that a dead monkey's hand, resting alongside a coffee mug, had been used "as an ashtray" on the research director's desk.

Recollections of Alex Pacheco's undercover investigation as told to Anna Francione appear in the book *In Defense of Animals,* edited by Peter Singer (Harper & Row, 1986). Describing vivisection, Pacheco said, "I saw discolored, exposed muscle tissue on their arms...bones protruding their flesh. Several had bitten off their own fingers and had festering stubs...they searched through ...waste pans for something to eat."

According to papers released to the press by PETA, the experiments involving the Silver Spring Monkeys were funded by a grant from the National Institute of Health for $300,000. In 1984, however, another vivisector was

51

receiving nearly $1 million a year from NIH "to simulate with baboons the kinds of head injuries human beings receive in boxing matches, football games, and car accidents," according to a PETA casework report.

A secret underground group, known as the Animal Liberation Front (ALF), broke into the laboratory of the head-injury clinic, removed more than sixty hours of video-tapes, and anonymously gave copies of the tapes to PETA. The report issued by PETA on the head-injury clinic states that the injured baboons' heads were cut open for exam-ination without proper anesthesia. According to the report, one baboon is seen attempting to lift his head while being cut open and another while being subjected to painful electro-cautery. The report further quotes several of the vivisectors adding insult to injury by ridiculing their vic-tims with attempts at sardonic humor: "The video camera pans across to another severely injured baboon slumped in a chair and staring with her mouth sagging open and drooling. A researcher announces that 'cheerleading over here in the corner we have B-10 [staff members are heard laughing]. . . B-10 wishes her counterpart well.' "

The following year, more than 100 animal-rights activists engaged in civil disobedience by occupying an entire floor of NIH for seventy-seven consecutive hours until then-Secretary of Health and Human Services Margaret M. Heckler agreed to shut down the laboratory by revoking the grant.

Later in 1985, ALF broke into another research laboratory to rescue more than 100 animals. In doing so, ALF members also removed documents and took photographs to provide evidence that the animals had been living in squalid conditions. The evidence was again anonymously turned over to PETA. As a result, NIH temporarily suspended more than $1 million of its federal grant funds and the U.S. Department of Agriculture imposed an $11,000 fine on the vivisector. The PETA casework report stated that more than half of the animals housed in the facility died of drug overdoses, improper anesthesia, bronchial bleeding, pulmonary infection, and a type of poisoning that a medical textbook described as "usually the work of ignorant pranksters" because the poison—croton oil—has "no therapeutic use." Among the animals secretly removed by ALF was an infected mother bloodhound without milk to feed her pups, who lay dead and dying amidst piles of excrement.

Still in 1985, ALF struck again, this time rescuing 467 animals being used in sight-deprivation and other cruel studies. According to the PETA casework report culled from the material given it, NIH had awarded more than $4 million to experiment on 5,000 animals, putting the sight-deprivation experiments on "minimal funding" of $10,000 a month.

The subsequent NIH investigation came to the conclusion that there were no deficiencies, but this excerpt from the PETA report about an infant monkey named Britches tells another story: "Britches was found. . . with his eyes sewn shut and a bulky sonar device taped crudely to his tiny head. He had been torn away from his mother at birth, and was kept isolated with no source of nour-ishment or comfort except a pipe with a plastic nipple." The report indicated that the portion of funding devoted to sight-deprivation experiments on animals was at least $275,000—money that could have easily been used in rehabilitation programs for humans instead of destructive

The Animal Liberation Front (ALF) frees cats from a laboratory.
(Photo courtesy of ALF)

ALF strikes again, this time rescuing dogs from a research laboratory.
(Photo courtesy of ALF)

programs for animals.

In 1987, PETA was sent a videotape that showed a medical-school dog laboratory in progress. As a result of the public outcry over release of the videotape, many medical schools have subsequently halted their dog labs. The PETA casework report provides an inside look at vivisection in action:

> As the instructor begins to cut the dog open, the dog whines—an obvious indication that he feels the pain of the incision. . . . The second instructor cut open the dog's chest, tore the chest open with his hands and cut the dog's ribs with garden shears . . . The heart rate of a properly sedated dog is 80–120 beats per minute; the tape shows this dog's heart rate was nearly 200—a sign that his level of consciousness was high enough for him to experience pain.

It was during the following year that PETA received videotapes of perhaps the most incomprehensible vivisection imaginable: a series of inexplicable university experiments in which mice, rats, and rabbits are placed in a bathtub for slaughter by a ferret. The PETA casework report that developed out of this incident displays a photograph of a ferret devouring a mouse, with a caption that reads: "The piercing screams of the pursued animals lasted for several minutes." Another photo showed a ferret doing to the same to a rabbit. The caption says: "It took more than nine excruciating minutes for the ferret to kill this rabbit."

ALF celebrated Independence Day in 1989 by breaking into a laboratory and freeing five surviving cats from a

Another animal from a laboratory is liberated by ALF.
(Photo courtesy of ALF)

This dog would have been tortured to death were it not for ALF.
(Photo courtesy of ALF)

series of experiments dating back to 1973 that had garnered more than $800,000 in NIH grants. Once again, PETA anonymously received evidence taken during the break-in, which it presented in its casework report: "The results revealed that closure [of the eye] was a complex process consisting of a series of simultaneous downward movements of the upper lid and that this closure was necessarily, in part, an active process."

To the cats involved in the experiments it was no laughing matter. According to the report, the top of a cat's skull was removed and steel screws were cemented into the bony orbit surrounding the eye so that wire electrodes could be implanted directly into the cat's brains. One experiment conditioned cats not to breathe at the sound of a tone or be subjected to a spray of irritating vapor in their faces.

In 1990, PETA released results of its own undercover investigation of companies that supply preserved animals to schools for dissection. A caption under one photograph speaks volumes: "Cats tossed onto tables after being killed." The horror stories are too numerous to recount.

The assumptions behind vivisection are immoral. The irrelevance and redundancy are wasteful. But, most important of all, vivisection is unconstitutional. When Amendment VIII was added to the United States Constitution in 1791, no restriction was placed on species to the prohibition that "cruel and unusual punishments [shall not be] inflicted." The United States government sponsors vivisection, and it is the most cruel and unusual punishment the world has ever known. It is inevitable that a compassionate Supreme Court will someday outlaw it. But that day will never come until enough people throw their support behind the animal-rights movement to push the issue through the judicial process.

Experiencing intolerable pain and immeasurable damage, if not death, from taking part in a scientific experiment is something that most compassionate people would not even wish on a Saddam Hussein- or Ted Bundy-like person, a person for whom "sadistic" would be too mild a description. Most Americans like, even love, animals. Yet American society accepts the reality of subjecting innocent animals to intolerable pain, immeasurable damage, and a violent death for medical research under the premise that the research is both necessary and beneficial. The irony is that it is not.

The fact that vivisection is not medically necessary any longer is evident in a letter sent by Dr. Neal Barnard to prospective members of the Physicians Committee for Responsible Medicine. Dr. Barnard, who chairs the committee, explains how "effective alternative methods can and have been used to teach physicians and conduct research without inflicting pain and death on animals." Dr. Barnard presents these alternatives in a series of rhetorical questions. In the words of Dr. Barnard:

> Did you know, for example, that simulators and computer models can be far more useful as teaching tools for medical students than operating on innocent animals? Did you know that scientists can now test potential anti-cancer drugs on actual human cancer cells rather than on animals? Or that vaccines can now be produced in cell cultures rather than on animals?

A PETA fact sheet on methods alternative to vivisection cites as among the most important the use of "human volunteers, clinical case studies, autopsy reports, and statistical analysis linked with clinical observation of disease." The use of human volunteers in clinical surveys entails observation of existing conditions rather than the creation of a condition, which is the case with vivisection. Instead of breaking a dog's limbs to observe them being reset, for the purpose of learning how to treat humans, the actual resetting of a human's broken bone can be videotaped.

Not only is vivisection immoral, wasteful, and unnecessary, it is also inconclusive. Who is to say that improved sanitation and better nutrition have not had as much to do with increased human life spans as the use of animals in medical research?

The unreliability of vivisection can set off a chain reaction of events that compound the negative effects of its limitations. When that happens, the immorality and waste become a hazard as well. In a report published by People for Reason in Science and Medicine, Dr. Roy Kupsinel explodes the myth of animal research and its values to human health. He points out that "aspirin and Tylenol kill cats, penicillin kills guinea pigs, Advil and Motrin cause severe gastric problems in dogs, Dristan is harmful to cats, [and] eyedrops can cause blindness in animals."

Dr. Kupsinel also points out that safe use has been demonstrated through vivisection for PCP as a horse tranquilizer, poisonous mushrooms for rabbits, prussic acid for porcupines, arsenic for sheep, and cyanide for owls. It was exhaustive animal testing that gave doctors confidence in

Thalidomide, which produced the most grotesque birth defects imaginable in humans. Imagine what might have transpired if falsified data had been used in the studies of Thalidomide. The chain of events that might have followed are chilling, but no more chilling than what really happened when the product was tested on animals and found to be safe for humans.

The issue of falsified data is real. A column by Jack Anderson and Dale Van Atta that appeared in the September 6, 1990, issue of the *Washington Post* revealed that the Justice Department joined a private lawsuit against one researcher "accused of falsifying reports in connection with $1.2 million in grants" from NIH. The researcher was "alleged to have faked the results of his study on how the human immune system is affected by burn injuries." Anderson and Van Atta estimated that more than $6 million in federal research money is under scrutiny at any given time by the NIH Office of Scientific Integrity over allegations of scientific fraud.

Scientific fraud is impossible to detect. The only way my dissertation committee could have provided absolute verification as to the authenticity of research leading toward a Ph.D. would have been to virtually duplicate the research I had done. Pressures to complete a study, compounded by the lure of prominence for having produced research findings worthy of publication, create a temptation to commit scientific fraud. It is hoped that vivisectors do not fake results in their research. The chain reaction of waste and faulty assumptions that would result from scientific fraud—when added to inferences derived from the quantum leap of transferring knowledge gained about animals to human—makes animal research inconclusive at best.

On March 26, 1991, Abigail Trafford reported in a *Washington Post* feature article that the NIH Office of Scientific Integrity had settled 100 cases and that an additional 70 allegations of scientific fraud were under investigation; as well as that several scientists were found to have falsified data. According to Trafford: "In only one case did the whistle-blower knowingly bring false charges against a colleague. . . . Nonetheless, even the best-intentioned whistleblower is usually made to pay."

The April 1, 1991, issue of *Newsweek* put the issue of scientific fraud in these blunt terms: "When researchers make up data on which treatment for retarded children is based (to which one researcher pleaded guilty in 1988), or when they accept fees from or hold stock in manufacturers whose drugs they test, then people's health and lives can be jeopardized."

In the Summer/Fall 1990 issue of the National Association of Nurses Against Vivisection newsletter, Nurse Betsy Todd wrote: "This is not a matter of the interests of humans versus the interests of animals. . . It is the economic interest of the biomedical research community that is pitted against the health interests of the general public."

Sometimes, as Betsy Todd illustrated, animal research gives the illusion of importance; but even with the advantage of source credibility inherent in medical credentials, vivisection cannot hold up under close scrutiny. Consider, for example, the case reported in the August 30–September 12 issue of *Everybody's News,* a local Cincinnati newspaper, in which a team of Florida doctors made a bid for grant dollars in the early 1980s "to drown forty-two. . .dogs in an attempt to prove the Heimlich Maneuver inadequate for drowning victims." Dr. Henry Heimlich, expressing his opposition to the $20,000 research grant, was quoted in the paper as saying, "It had already been proven by humans saved using the technique that the Heimlich Maneuver was working. Why would it be necessary to put the dogs through 'cruel' and 'useless' experiments only to come to the same conclusion?" To Dr. Heimlich's logic, reporter Katina A. Jones added this aside: "How do you perform mouth-to-mouth resuscitation on a dog?"

All of this lends credence to a large black button I was given by Tony Promutico, of the Maryland Forum for Animals. The button conveyed a very disturbing message, but one that is becoming increasingly apparent. In bright white letters, the button reads: "Animal Research Is Scientific Fraud."

Oliver is shown here in the arms of Candice Bergen. It is hard to believe the agony that Oliver would have experienced had he not been rescued on his way to a laboratory for vivisection.
(Photo courtesy of PETA)

This is what an animal researcher apparently considers science: a monkey strapped in bondage. If this photo resembles pornography, that is because it is. (Photo courtesy of PETA)

And this is what an animal researcher apparently considers an ashtray: the amputated hand of a monkey. It is difficult to imagine what must go through an animal researcher's mind.
(Photo courtesy of PETA)

Rabbits used in the Draize Eye Irritancy Test are put into restraining devices with only their heads protruding. The substance being tested is dripped into their eyes. The animals scream and sometimes break their necks as they struggle to escape. (Photo courtesy of PETA)

When Grace Slick wrote the classic hit "White Rabbit" and sang it in the 1960s as a member of the Jefferson Airplane (later Jefferson Starship), she had no idea that white rabbits were being tortured in laboratories to protect companies from liability suits. As an animal-rights activist in the 1990s, "White Rabbit" undoubtedly has a different meaning to her now. Standing behind Grace is her daughter, China Kantner, famous in her own right as MTV VJ and KRQR DJ. (Photo by Johnson Studios, courtesy of Grace Slick and China Kantner)

Chapter 4

Product Testing on Animals

*I*f vivisection is the act of cutting into live animals for money or scientific curiosity, then doing it primarily to satisfy officials of the Food and Drug Administration that each ingredient in a commercial product is considered adequately substantiated for safety may appropriately be called "vivitution," because it comes even closer to prostitution.

Testing products on animals is the cheapest way for companies to escape having to include warning statements on product labels to indicate that safety has not been determined; and it is substantially cheaper than having to restrict the contents of products to ingredients and combinations of ingredients that have already been determined to be safe.

At least in vivisection there is a pretense of destroying animals for a purpose other than money; in vivitution there is none. Though you won't find the word "vivitution" in any dictionary, you will find the ravaging effects of vivitution in nearly every product you use that does not bear a marking that it has not been tested on animals.

Many shoppers would not buy their usual brand of laundry detergent, if they only knew. They would not buy many of the products that sit on their shelves at home, if they only knew—if they only knew what for many years

65

has been the best-kept secret in business. It was the animal-rights movement that brought product testing on animals to media attention. Until then, few people realized that they had patronized the torture of animals by purchasing products that had been tested on animals.

The issue of testing products on animals gained national press coverage in 1985, when PETA released photographs taken by Leslie Fain, who had courageously blown the whistle on the company that employed her. The photographs showed the results of acute dermal toxicity tests, in which bare skin was scraped raw for the application of toxic substances. She had been inspired by Alex Pacheco's undercover investigation of the Silver Spring Monkeys; and, as a result, she too emerged as a heroic defender of animals' rights.

In letters signed by Pacheco, PETA quoted from Fain's diary to promote a national boycott of that company's products. Some of the excerpts from Leslie Fain's diary read:

> Technicians laughed while they put...shaving cream...in rabbits' eyes and callously force-fed ...deodorant to animals in death tests....Regardless of whether or not the rabbit was dead, they would throw it approximately 10 feet onto a pile ...Many rabbits would still be crawling...on top of the dead and other dying rabbits....Blood was coming out of some of their mouths; others were convulsing and having spasms.

PETA attacked from all fronts. In the April 16, 1990, *Boston Business Journal*, John Glass reported how PETA had placed on stockholder proxy statements the question "Should the company disclose how many animals it uses for product safety testing?" and that "a second proposal on [the]...proxy statement, submitted by an individual, asks the company to halt animal testing altogether." Glass went on to report that PETA had 80 shares of that company's stock and over four years "had been gaining shareholder votes, from 3 percent the first year to 9.9 percent."

Concern over potential media exposure of organized boycotts has resulted in a growing number of pledges from companies never to test their products on animals again, and fear of animal-rights whistle-blowers or undercover agents from animal-rights organizations on their payrolls have no doubt resulted in at least partial, if not full, compliance with those pledges. Nevertheless, according to PETA fact sheets on the subject, an estimated 14 million✓ animals suffer and die each year in gruesome tests on every conceivable type of commercial product. This is how the PETA fact sheet describes what happens when a product is tested on animals: "Substance is dropped into the eyes of...rabbits.... They usually receive no anesthesia...for a 72-hour period...during [which] the rabbits' eyelids are held open with clips, and their ineffective tear ducts prevent them from blinking or washing away the substance." This is known as the Draize Eye Irritancy Test. Companies also conduct acute toxicity tests to determine the amount of a substance that is required to kill an animal. The PETA fact sheet indicates that "the widely used Lethal Dose 50 (LD-50) test... continues until 50 percent of the animals die, usually in two to four weeks."

*I*t was the combined force of another undaunted whistle-blower and an undercover investigator from PETA that brought the spotlight inside an animal-testing laboratory used to determine the safety of cosmetic and household products. The PETA case work report on the laboratory charged not only "that animals are grossly unprotected from cruelty and abuse, but that the public is also unprotected by faulty and sometimes fraudulent testing practice."

Inside the animal-testing laboratory, the heroic whistle-blower watched with horror as rabbits were blinded with hairspray and guinea pigs were force-fed bath gel. She saw mice being roasted alive to test sunscreening lotion.

According to the PETA report, laboratory technicians not only acknowledged inaccuracies in their testing methodologies but also offered the obvious reason why companies test their products on animals. As one technician so succinctly put it, "The companies just do it to cover their butts." No matter how slim the pretense of scientific merit, the very existence of product research establishes some position of "good faith" for the company in the case of a law suit or other product-related liability.

An example was cited of a company paying the laboratory $1,500 to drown mice in cooking oil in defense of a consumer's complaint that a dead mouse had appeared in a bottle of oil that had been purchased and, possibly, used. When the whistle-blower contacted PETA, an undercover investigator became employed as a laboratory technician to verify the atrocities.

The agent found that some technicians were frequently found laughing at the screaming animals—and that there was falsified data. According to the casework report, "the agent was told to 'just write in' random scores on the data sheet."

It was in 1987 when the whistle-blower first contacted PETA. After the evidence was released to the public the following year, it had a powerful impact on the attitudes of companies both towards this research facility and animal testing, in general. Many companies not only stopped contracting with that laboratory to have their products tested on animals, but stopped testing their products on animals altogether. PETA also revealed the identity of the whistle-blower upon her request at that time. Cheryl Baker knew that defending animals' rights was always the right thing to do; and she did.

The proprietary nature of product testing legitimizes the cloak of secrecy intended to hide atrocities from the public with a pretense of hiding trade secrets from competitors. For this reason, a typical experiment is apt to be repeated by any number of companies with virtually identical products to test. In addition to the obvious immorality, product testing on animals imposes a staggering cost on the consumer that is without any benefit.

But the cloak of secrecy put up by companies around product testing on animals is not nearly as covert as that which conceals weapons testing on animals by the military. In the cover story of the September 1989 issue of *Penthouse*, author Jack Rosenberger revealed that promises made by the Department of Defense to members of Congress "that it would not shoot dogs or cats for any form of ballistic research" had been ignored; there was, in fact, one $2 million grant for experiments in which live cats were being shot in the head as proof.

Paul and Linda McCartney, shown here on the PETA catalog cover,
have taken an aggressive stand to promote animals' rights. The PETA
catalog offers products that have not been tested on animals.
(Photo courtesy of PETA)

Rosenberger writes that a group of eighteen physicians and other medical experts who had reviewed the researchers' work concluded "that it is extremely unlikely [the]...experiments will ever yield any data helpful to humans." Military testing of products on animals has been the object of frustration to many activists in the animal-rights movement, as demonstrated by a distinct pattern of denials to their Freedom of Information Act requests on the dubious basis of remotely related exemptions to the law.

In assessing the uselessness of vivitution, the only thing of relevance to humans that is learned is not how products are tested on animals; it is how animals are tested on products.

In acute dermal toxicity tests, the hair is shaved from each animal's abdomen and back. Guinea pigs and rabbits are most often used. Half of the animals receive abrasions deep enough to penetrate the outer layer of their skin. The test substance is then applied and covered with a rubber sleeve. Inflammation, poisoning, even death may result, depending on the strength of the substance. (Photo courtesy of PETA)

Dr. Tom Regan, author of *The Case for Animal Rights,* leads a protest against veal. (Photo courtesy of FARM)

Peter Singer (left), whose *Animal Liberation* is considered the bible of animals' rights, with Dr. Alex Hershaft, founder of Farm Animal Reform Movement (FARM). (Photo courtesy of FARM)

72

Chapter 5

The Factory Farming of Animals

A lex Hershaft, founder of the Farm Animal Reform Movement, traces his fight against factory farming to his early experiences in the Warsaw ghetto. Factory farming refers to the cruel practice of cramming as many animals in as small a space as possible to maximize the number of animals raised on a given farm. Dr. Hershaft quotes Isaac Bashevis Singer's portrayal of humans: "They have convinced themselves that man, the worst transgressor of all the species, is the crown of creation. All other creatures were created merely to provide him with food, pelts, to be tormented, experimented. [To animals]. . . all people are Nazis; for the animals, it is an eternal Treblinka."

The initials of Hershaft's group, not coincidentally, form the acronym FARM. Its literature describes factory farming as follows:

Veal calves are torn from their mothers at birth, chained by the neck in tiny crates without bedding or light, unable to turn around or scratch, and forced to stand or lie for 16 weeks on wood slats

Top: Dr. Alex Hershaft conducts civil disobedience on behalf
of FARM. Bottom: FARM members doing same.
(Photos courtesy of FARM)

PETA's Cam MacQueen joins forces with FARM to protest veal.
(Photo courtesy of FARM)

covered with their excrement. . . . Breeding sows
are kept continuously pregnant and confined in tiny
metal "gestation stalls." . . . Laying hens are
crammed up to five birds in a tiny "battery cage"
the size of a folded newspaper.

In a flyer announcing the site of demonstrations for the
1990 World Farm Animals Day, Hershaft wrote, "Confinement, deprivation, mutilation, and premature slaughter are
the way of life and death for nearly five billion farm
animals in the United States each year. . . . The U.S.
Department of Agriculture has consistently opposed any

Marchers protest factory farming. (Photo courtesy of FARM)

Peter Link Gerrard, of the National Alliance, who organized the
historic March on Washington in 1990, pauses with Dr. Tom Regan,
author of the classic book *The Case for Animal Rights.* (Photo by
Scott D. Christopher; courtesy of National Alliance for Animal Legislation)

legislation designed to improve the conditions of farm animals and failed to enforce the few existing laws."

A PETA pamphlet on the subject provides further examples of factory farming:

> Cattle are dehorned, castrated, and branded without anesthetics. Some dairy cows spend their entire lives in tiny stalls, plagued by repeated artificial insemination and near-constant pregnancy. . . . Overcrowding breeds disease; and factory farmers routinely spray animals with pesticides and dose them with antibiotics and other drugs.

The issue of factory farming has caused a few activists, operating independently, to lose their patience with farmers in the Midwest. The October 2, 1990, issue of the *Journal Star*, Peoria, Illinois, reported that farmers in the Midwest had allegedly experienced "harassing phone calls and letters, overturned cattle hutches, burned hay barns, and equipment tampering." An article by Clare Howard, from the same issue, alleged that "in increasing numbers, livestock farmers are being targeted by animal-rights groups, which are becoming more active in protesting the ways all animals are treated. . . . Farmers are reluctant to publicly talk about vandalism for fear of raising their profile, thus increasing their vulnerability."

The 1985 book of readings *In Defense of Animals*, edited by Peter Singer (Harper & Row), excerpted an article by Dr. Tom Regan that put the issue of factory farming into perspective. "Giving farm animals more space," he wrote, "more natural environments, more companions does not right the fundamental wrong any more than giving lab

"Factory farm animals never have a nice day" expresses the reason why these animal rights activists are protesting the slaughterhouse atrocities. (Photos courtesy of FARM)

animals more anesthesia or bigger, cleaner cages would right the fundamental wrong in their case. Nothing less than the total dissolution of commercial animal agriculture will do this, just as . . . morality requires nothing less than the total elimination of hunting and trapping for commercial and sporting ends."

Just as the atrocities of hunting and slaughterhouses have made many people vegetarians, the atrocities of factory farming have made many vegetarians vegans— meaning that dairy products as well as meat are excluded from their diets.

Dr. Alex Hershaft leads protest against hot-iron branding of dairy cows.
(Photos courtesy of FARM)

79

The nonchalance of Ann Chynoweth (left) and Franklin Maphis
(right) evokes memories of the old television series *Three's Company*,
in that something very unusual was taking place with this trio that was
not apparent to bystanders. Ann and Franklin were chained by their
ankles to the knees of Heidi Prescott (center), who was chained to the
fence behind. This company of three stalled the opening of a 1989
hunt at the Mason Neck National Wildlife Refuge in Virginia for
three hours before police could unlock their chains.
(Photo courtesy of PETA)

Chapter 6

Hunting

*H*unting is the heated anticipation and obsessive pursuit of a brief but passionate feeling of pleasure derived by randomly selecting defenseless animals and murdering them. A hunter is a serial killer licensed to act out violent fantasies on selected species.

Many hunters rationalize that they hunt to feed their families. But in reality the time expended in pursuit of animals to shoot makes hunting for food so uneconomical and inefficient that it sounds not only immoral but unintelligent as well.

Some hunters contend that they shoot animals to prevent them from starving to death, when in fact they typically ravage a species by killing off its healthiest members; and if a healthy *mother* is shot, her young may likely suffer a slow death of neglect.

In addition to the devastating ecological effects, the majority of animals shot linger in agony before they die.

Some hunters even contend that they kill animals in self-defense—as if they just happened to find themselves in the woods and armed with guns when encountering animals about to attack them. The real reason hunters hunt is because killing humans is illegal.

At a pre-dawn protest sponsored by The Fund for Animals, hunters
are met by defenders of animals' rights.
(Photo courtesy of PETA)

The ludicrousness of viewing hunting as a sport was
subtly captured by a television commercial in 1991. The
commercial begins with a nervous whisper, and then a
deer is spotted. She helplessly looks directly toward the
millions of viewers, who instinctively brace as the nervous
whisper of an accomplice advises what presumably is
another hunter to shoot. There is a chilling click—and
finally a photograph appears. The commercial is for a

camera. But the illusion of vicariously murdering a deer is indelible.

Patterns of inexplicable court rulings suggest that hunters are granted immunity for their crimes against nature and a presumption of having been impugned when their right to kill is questioned. In some states, animal-rights activists have been fined and even jailed for making noise that might scare animals off to safety under hunter harassment laws. But perhaps the most incredulous court ruling was reported in the October 18, 1990, issue of the *New York Times* in a story that went largely unnoticed because of simultaneous events in the Persian Gulf.

According to the *Times,* Karen Wood, a 37-year-old mother of twins, had moved to Maine just four months before a man would shoot her dead. The man was found innocent of manslaughter because he mistook her not for a burglar, but for a sweet and innocent deer. According to the article, the man "saw what he thought was the white underside of a deer's tail and fired. . . . Mrs. Wood was wearing white mittens when she was killed. . . . Some people. . .suggested that Mrs. Wood was at fault for wearing the mittens when it was hunting season." It is a wonder that no posthumous charges were brought against the woman for having worn white mittens in the vicinity of the hunter. Only because the man mistakenly thought he had shot a deer was he found not guilty of killing a woman.

That same month, Joy Williams published an article in *Esquire* magazine. The article presented an incisive case against hunting. In her words, "Hunters get a thrill out of seeing a plummeting bird, out of seeing it crumble and fall. . . . The excitement of shooting [a] bear had Barb talking a mile a minute."

The number of drunken hunters who accidentally shoot themselves is also staggering. But how can one be sorry when a hunter has been shot? He has killed so many times before; and now he cannot.

Even as a young man, my father would not hunt—"because the animals cannot shoot back."

It was in the January 1989 issue of *The Animals' Agenda* that the mental health of hunters was most succinctly addressed. In an interview with Wayne Pacelle, Luke Dommer, Chairperson of the Committee to Abolish Sport Hunting, stated, "Many hunters are sick people. . . . In Massachusetts, five hunters returning from an unsuccessful hunt saw a puppy tied outside and opened fire on

84

the animal. In California, two hunters killed a black man on a railroad track, and they admitted in court that they did it because they didn't get anything else."

Roger Stevenson, Ann Chynoweth, Amy Bertsch, Jennifer Johnson, and Jenny Woods demonstrate what to say to a person who is wearing fur. (Photo courtesy of PETA)

The slogan on Cam MacQueen's shirt explains why. (Photo courtesy of PETA)

86

Chapter 7

Fur and Leather

Nothing could evoke more outrage than a coat made of human faces—the actual faces of human beings who had agonized for days in steel leghold traps before being stomped to death—humans who had been bred on a face ranch in horrendous conditions only to be anally electrocuted or even have their faces skinned while they were still alive.

Nothing could compare in callousness to the gloating of a person attired in such a coat over the 125 people who lost their lives to make it, or over the handsomeness and beauty of many of the faces on the coat. Suppose for a moment that you suddenly found yourself in a society in which expensive face coats were the height of fashion.

This, of course, would be a society that could only exist in the Twilight Zone, but imagine that a social movement has succeeded in making the public aware of the atrocities that went into making a face coat. Suddenly, face coats have been relegated from symbols of elegance, because of their prohibitive cost, to objects of contempt. Activists in the social movement frequently ridicule people wearing face coats; some even spit or throw blood upon face coats. Then, all at once, a person approaches you in friendly conversation. The person is wearing a face coat. What would you say, in that science-fictional context, to a person

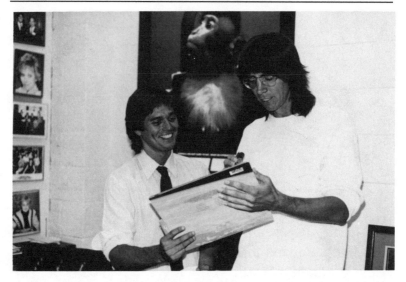

Alex Pacheco with Tom Scholz of the rock group Boston, who has sponsored musical events against fur. (Photo courtesy of PETA)

Cassandra "Elvira" Peterson has been a leader in the battle to ban fur. (Photo courtesy of PETA)

If you look just once into her eyes, you may never wear fur again.
(Photo courtesy of PETA)

wearing a face coat? The same thing *now* that you should say to a person wearing a fur coat.

This is what you should say: that the coat is a corpse, and you have been made ill looking at it. Instead of faces, fur coats are made of pelts—the entire skin of an animal with the fur still on it. The story, however, is still the same: from agonizing days in steel leghold traps until being stomped to death; from horrendous conditions at fur ranches to a deadly cycle of being bred, anally electrocuted, if not poisoned or gassed, and then skinned, possibly while still alive. The story is the same. Only the species has changed.

89

Singer Howard Jones and actress Mink Stole protest fur.
(Photo courtesy of PETA)

L. to R.: Kathy Valentine, Gina Schock, Belinda Carlisle, Jane
Wiedlin, and Charlotte Caffey. In May 1991, Jane Wiedlin joined the
PETA trio of Dan Mathews, Jenny Woods, and Ann Chynoweth in
stripping to their underwear to disrupt a major fur show in New
York. Their antics received major publicity; the fur show did not.
(Photo by Greg Gorman, courtesy of PETA)

According to *The Animals' Agenda* fact sheets on the subject, "approximately 3.8 million furbearing animals were trapped in 1989 in the United States . . . and another 4.5 million animals were raised on fur farms." Nonetheless, the animal-rights movement continues to erode the business of American furriers. The motto "Fur is dead" has now taken on a double meaning. The first is that the fur is part of a corpse, and the second is that the time for gaining social acceptance while wearing a fur garment has passed forever.

It is ironic that the same glamorous actresses and singers who brought prestige to fur coats are now the very ones who have taken the lead in discarding them. Certainly one of the most provocative demonstrations against fur came in the form of a 1990 poster that showed all five members of the female rock group "The Go-Go's" strategically posed behind a large PETA banner with their arms extended high in the air. In the middle was Belinda Carlisle, flanked on her right by Kathy Valentine and Gina Schock, and on her left by Jane Wiedlin and Charlotte Caffey. The banner, placed above the PETA logo, read: WE'D RATHER GO-GO NAKED THAN WEAR FUR.

Leaders of the animal-rights movement also prescribe the use of compassionate alternatives to leather products. According to PETA fact sheets, "skin accounts for 50 percent of the total by-product value of cattle . . . thus the economic success of the slaughterhouse (and the dairy farm) is directly linked to the sale of . . . leather." Ingrid Newkirk has frequently referred to leather as "hairless fur." Advances in techniques used to produce canvas and vinyl footwear have even made leather shoes unnecessary. In addition, the unnatural techniques used to produce wool and down cause suffering in sheep, ducks, and geese. That, too, prompts animal-rights activists to seek compassionate alternatives.

FARM President Alex Hershaft and Fund for Animals President Cleveland Amory grimace as they inspect a cow whose skin will eventually be used to make leather. (Photo courtesy of FARM)

This is a graphic look at the slogan "Fur Is Dead." When you slip
into a fur, you put on your body the corpses of dozens of animals—
animals who lost their lives for what you are wearing, like this one.
(Photo courtesy of PETA)

Heidi Prescott, seen here protesting meat, became the first animal-rights activist to be jailed under Maryland's hunter harassment laws. Her crime was rustling leaves to scare away endangered animals while a hunter was attempting to begin the deadly food cycle of meat. (Photo courtesy of FARM)

Chapter 8

Meat

*E*ating meat is part of a deadly food cycle that traps every participant and victim in its grim repetition The cycle begins with the chilling rhythm of animal claws on a slaughterhouse floor in a desperate struggle for a last gasp of breath, tapped out in harmony with shrieks from pain. This morbid music is part of the first stage of the meat-eating cycle: killing the animals. Over every other slaughterhouse noise you will hear the shrieks of the screaming victims, like a gruesome cacophonous chorus. Once you have been to a slaughterhouse, you cannot get the tapping claws and piercing cries out of your ears. The animals scream in piercing soprano voices, until they are dead. Butchers wade in a sea of blood.

Another form of meat is fish. Anyone who has ever witnessed a hooked fish squirming knows that fish feel pain too. The edible flesh of fish is not an alternative to meat; it *is* meat.

The cycle continues at a supermarket, where consumers buy their meat. Some pay high prices for the choicer cuts. These consumers do not buy lower-priced alternatives to meat. In this stage, the second stage, the human meat-eaters suffer economic victimization.

Then the meat is eaten. If this represents a pattern over a person's life, meat-eating humans may find themselves at the next stage, diagnosed with either heart trouble or

As long as Gene Bauston is around, Hamilton will never be meat on anyone's table. (Photo courtesy of Farm Sanctuary)

cancer. This victim of the meat-eating cycle then likely suffers a slow, excruciating struggle to stay alive. No fast or bloody end to his struggle, but instead a slow and uncertain future.

Like the animals in the slaughterhouse, he ultimately dies a needless death. The cycle is complete.

Two often-heard slogans among animal-rights activists are that "Meat Is Murder" and that "Meat Stinks." It is also fitting to add that "Meat Is for Morons." Eating meat is not only immoral; it is stupid. It is stupid because you can get the same necessary nutritional elements from foods other than meat. People fall into the deadly food cycle of eating meat by acquiring a taste for it through habit.

Habits, however, can always be changed; all it takes to break from the meat cycle is awareness of the revolting idea that you are eating dead flesh—and that it is disgusting as well as immoral. As eating habits change, so too does taste. People who go from the extremes of drowning their foods with catsup to not eating with any condiments on their foods at all generally lose their desire for catsup; the same is true of people who switch from salted to unsalted nuts. Former smokers generally find the passive smoke of others to be distasteful. Eating meat is a bad habit, but one that is easy to break. Vegetarian eating is more palatable, healthful, economical, and obviously more compassionate.

Celebrity entertainers from Paul McCartney to country music star K. D. Lang have joined forces with PETA in an effort to influence people to abstain from eating meat. McCartney has been quoted in PETA literature as saying, "We don't eat anything that has to be killed for us. We've reached a stage where we really value life." On a cover of one issue of *PETA News*, Lang is quoted as saying, "We all love animals; why do we call some 'pets' and others 'dinner'?"

K. D. Lang is right. It really is hypocritical to love one animal and eat another. When I celebrated my undergraduate degree here, with Buddy, I was betraying the love he felt for me by eating meat.
(Photo courtesy of Al Silverman)

(Photos courtesy of FARM)

A "vegan" diet is one that not only excludes meat but dairy products as well. In the November 4, 1990, issue of the *Saint Paul Pioneer Press,* reporter Mary Ann Grossman interviewed PETA National Director Ingrid Newkirk, who had been in that town on tour for her book *Save the Animals!* (Warner Books, 1990). Describing her conversion to a vegan diet, Newkirk said, "I became a vegan when I was a cruelty investigator and was sent on a particularly horrible case involving abandoned horses and pigs. Driving home that night, I was wondering what to have for supper and thought about pork chops. I realized I was trying to prosecute this grotesque crime while I was paying someone else to do the same thing at a slaughterhouse."

As Chairman of the Physicians Committee for Responsible Medicine, Dr. Neal Barnard put the issue of meat in clear and unambiguous terms: "Animal products are not necessary and indeed are harmful in the human diet." In the April 16, 1988, issue of the *Washington Post,* columnist Colman McCarthy quoted from the writings of Nobel laureate Isaac Bashevis Singer in concluding, "Those who eat meat share in the guilt."

(Photo courtesy of FARM)

Chapter 9

Animals in Sport and Entertainment

*M*ost people can immediately recognize the suffering endured by animals in bullfighting, but they tend to overlook the suffering and deaths inflicted upon animals through forced participation in horse racing, dog racing, rodeos, circuses, movies, and television shows.

Sometimes the suffering and deaths of these animals come as a result of increased risk inherent in the activity, sometimes as a result of intentional abuse. According to PETA fact sheets, "each year about 2,000 horses are injured on the track and must be euthanized." Moreover, the "American Association of Equine Practitioners veterinarians have labelled 60 to 90 percent of racehorses 'significantly lame.' " Dog racing is just as cruel. PETA fact sheets indicate that "dogs who slow down and become unprofitable are either killed or sold to research laboratories."

The November 5, 1990 issue of *Sports Illustrated* showed chilling photographs taken by Bill Frakes, which accompanied the article "Requiem at Belmont" by William Nack. Wrote Nack: "On a calamitous Breeders' Cup day, the champion filly Go for Wand snapped her right foreleg, fell to the track, and had to be destroyed." Undoubtedly, the lack of public interest over racing dogs leaves questions regarding the frequency of fatal injuries in that so-called sport unanswered.

The cover story of the March 1990 issue of *The Animals' Agenda* uncovered this little known fact about rodeos: "In the past three years in northern California (alone), there have been documented deaths of at least five animals due to injuries suffered in rodeos."

A local northern Virginia paper, the *Sun Gazette,* reported allegations in its October 11, 1990, issue of heroic barn hand Joanna Moore that an elephant trainer severely beat a tortoise. The paper quoted Moore as stating that the trainer "took a board . . . and started 'whacking' . . . When the tortoise tried to hide its head, Moore said (the trainer) started 'ramming the tortoise's face' (with the board). . . Moore said she wrenched the board from him, but saw that Jethro's (the tortoise's) nostrils were bleeding." This was a behind-the-scenes look at a zoo that few people would want to see.

The Animals' Agenda cover story for November 1989 revealed secrets of circus life for animals. This excerpt tells the story: " 'I really feel sorry for the tigers,' says another circus observer. 'Think how you'd feel if you had to spend all your life in one little spot, and the only time you got out was when you did the show. And the elephants, they're always chained. Just like prisoners.' "

The November/December 1990 issue of *PETA News* provided a typical example of how animals are abused in movies and in television. This is what PETA reported, on one movie, *Problem Child*: "Previews . . . showed a sociopathic child who spins the family cat in a washing machine, breaks his legs, and throws him across a room."

The use of animals in entertainment has no sport or entertainment in store for the animals; nor do aquariums. In a widely circulated letter dated April 2, 1991, veterinarians Wendy Thacher and Bob Potter protested the choice of the National Aquarium for a dinner sponsored by a veterinary medical association. In the words of Dr. Thacher and Dr. Potter, this is why: "Dolphins can live to be forty years old in the wild, yet rarely live beyond five years in captivity. . . ."

What you don't see when animals are used in entertainment is best represented by two photographs in the July/August 1990 *PETA News.* In the first photograph, an elephant is shown standing on its front legs. The second photograph shows the elephant lying on its side. It had crashed to the pavement. The same sickening thud accompanying that elephant's unnecessary fall is heard when overworked carriage horses collapse in the middle of a street. Many of them never get back up.

(Photo courtesy of PETA)

Declaration of The Rights of Animals

Whereas It Is Self-Evident

That we share the earth with other creatures, great and small;
That many of these animals experience pleasure and pain;
That these animals deserve our just treatment; and
That these animals are unable to speak for themselves;

We Do Therefore Declare That These Animals

HAVE THE RIGHT to live free from human exploitation, whether in the name of science or sport, exhibition or service, food or fashion;

HAVE THE RIGHT to live in harmony with their nature rather than according to human desires; and

HAVE THE RIGHT to live on a healthy planet.

THIS DECLARATION OF THE RIGHTS OF ANIMALS,
ADOPTED AND PROCLAIMED
ON THIS, THE TENTH DAY OF JUNE 1990,
IN WASHINGTON, D.C.

Declaration of the Rights of Animals Endorsing Organizations

American Fund for Alternatives to Animal Research • Albert Schweitzer Council for Animals and the Environment • American Anti-Vivisection Society • The American Society for the Prevention of Cruelty to Animals • Animal Legal Defense Fund • Animal Protection Institute • Animal Rights International • Animal Rights Mobilization • The Animals' Agenda • The Animals' Voice Magazine • Association of Veterinarians for Animal Rights • Beauty Without Cruelty, USA • CHAI • Compassion for Animals Foundation • Culture and Animals Foundation • Disabled and Incurably Ill for Alternatives to Animal Research • Doris Day Animal League • EcoVision • Farm Animal Reform Movement • Farm Sanctuary • Feminists for Animal Rights • Focus on Animals • Friends of Animals • The Fund for Animals • Gaia Institute • In Defense of Animals • International Network for Religion and Animals • International Primate Protection League • International Society for Animal Rights • Jews for Animal Rights • National Alliance for Animal Legislation • National Anti-Vivisection Society • National Humane Education Society • New England Anti-Vivisection Society • North Carolina Network for Animals • People for the Ethical Treatment of Animals • Performing Animals Welfare Society • Physicians Committee for Responsible Medicine • Primarily Primates • Psychologists for the Ethical Treatment of Animals • United Action for Animals • United Animal Nations—USA

(Photo courtesy of National Alliance for Animal Legislation)

Chapter 10

The Animal-Rights Philosophy Index

*T*o see how far your animal-rights philosophy has evolved, simply mark the item that best describes how you would most likely react in each of the following ten situations:

1. You hear on the radio that the National Institutes of Health (NIH) released research findings that analysis of brain tissue from 3,000 decapitated rabbits showed no significant increase in brain damage among those injected with a potential cancer-fighting drug; and that plans were being made to repeat the experiment with other drugs.

   a. You would pay no attention to the news report.

   b. You would write letters to your elected representatives to encourage the raising of additional funds for the experiments.

   c. You would write letters of protest to your elected representatives, demanding that the experiments be stopped.

"...the philosophy...that animals do not have immortal souls has the extraordinary consequence that they do not have consciousness either...They experience neither pleasure nor pain...Although they may squeal when cut with a knife, or writhe in their efforts to escape contact with a hot iron."

—Peter Singer,
from his book, *Animal Liberation*

"And God said, Let us make man...have dominion over the fish of the sea, and over the fowl of the air, and over the cattle, and over all the earth, and over every creeping thing that creepeth upon the earth."

—*Genesis*, The First Book of Moses

"The word 'dominion' refers to man's shepherding role, which denotes a guarantee and protection of animals' rights."

—Rabbi Harold S. White,
President of the International Network
for Religion and Animals
and Jewish Chaplin and Lecturer in Theology,
Georgetown University

     d. You would write letters of protest to your elected representatives, demanding that the experiments be stopped, and participate in any demonstrations organized by animal-rights groups at NIH.

2. You see a film exposing the miserable conditions that cows endure in factory farming.

     a. You would be inspired by the efficient manner in which milk is drawn.

     b. You would no longer consume dairy products.

     c. You would find the film incredibly boring.

     d. You would no longer consume dairy products and attempt to influence others not to consume dairy products.

3. A flyer from an animal-rights group encourages a boycott of a particular company that tests its cosmetic products on animals.

     a. You would intentionally purchase cosmetic products that are manufactured by that company.

     b. You would honor the boycott by not purchasing any of that company's products.

     c. You would pay no attention to the flyer or to the boycott it was intended to encourage.

     d. You would honor the boycott by not purchasing any of that company's products and encourage others to do the same.

4. You observe a neighbor repeatedly kicking his dog.

   a. You would mind your own business and look the other way.

   b. You would warn the neighbor that further abuse of his companion animal will result in a formal complaint by you to local authorities.

   c. You would confiscate the dog and find it a better home.

   d. You would join in with a few kicks of your own.

5. Your mother greets you at her door wearing a fur coat. The two of you are expected at a party across town.

   a. You would request that she change her coat as a favor to you, if not out of respect for animals— especially the animals her coat represents.

   b. You would tell her that she must change her coat in order to ride with you to the party.

   c. You would make no mention of her coat.

   d. You would tell her that the coat makes her look more attractive and encourage her to buy more fur products.

6. Your local newspaper exposes secret experiments that are being conducted at a nearby laboratory by the United States government to test the effect of music on pain tolerance. Dogs are being tortured to death and insanity by the hundreds, with high-volume classical music pumped directly into the dogs' ears.

   a. You would pay no attention to the newspaper article.

b. You would write letters of protest to your elected representatives, demanding that the experiments be stopped.

c. You would participate in demonstrations of protest.

d. You would write letters encouraging additional research on the subject.

7. You read a magazine article that describes gory details of how cows, fish, and chickens are slaughtered to make food for humans.

a. You develop a craving for a buffet of their flesh.

b. You would adhere to a strict vegetarian diet.

c. You would discard the magazine article without reading it.

d. You would adhere to a strict vegetarian diet and encourage others to do the same.

8. You receive a birthday gift of new shoes, a wallet, and a belt—all made of vinyl—along with a note requesting that you dispose of any leather shoes, wallets, and belts that you may have, out of respect for the cows which are slaughtered to make them.

a. You would continue to use and purchase leather products.

b. You would continue using what leather products you have, but stop purchasing new leather products.

c. You would no longer use or purchase leather products and encourage others to make the same change in their lives.

d. You would attempt to have a store exchange the vinyl gifts for leather products.

9. An animal-rights group organizes a demonstration at the Pentagon protesting that cats are being shot by members of the military services as part of ballistic-wound research conducted by the Department of Defense. You are there. Several of the protesters set themselves up for arrest by civil disobedience. Numerous television cameras are recording the event.

   a. You would chant animal-rights slogans along with the protesters.

   b. You would leave the demonstration site as quickly as possible.

   c. You would chant animal-rights slogans along with the protesters and participate in the civil disobedience.

   d. You would try to shout down and intimidate the protesters.

10. Your prospective father-in-law tries on his new hunting attire for you and asks for your opinion regarding how he looks in it.

    a. You would diplomatically avoid offering an opinion.

    b. You would tell him that you are against hunting.

    c. You would tell him that he looks like a mass murderer.

    d. You would tell him that he looks terrific.

Plotting Your Score

To determine how far your philosophy on animals' rights has evolved, find the column in Figure I under which the item you selected as your most probable reaction for each situation falls. For example, item (c) falls under the Defend column for the fourth situation about a neighbor repeatedly kicking his dog.

Figure I

Animal-Rights Philosophy
Represented by Items Selected

Situation	Exploit	Ignore	Respect	Defend
1	B	A	C	D
2	A	C	B	D
3	A	C	B	D
4	D	A	B	C
5	D	C	A	B
6	D	A	B	C
7	A	C	B	D
8	D	A	B	C
9	D	B	A	C
10	D	A	B	C

Beside your item selected for each situation, write the name of the animal-rights philosophy it represents. For example, in situation number 3, regarding the boycotting of a company that tests its cosmetic products on animals, the philosophy of respecting animals' rights is represented by item (b). Next to item (b), write "Respect" if that was your response.

Each of the four philosophies carries a weighted value for plotting on a four-quadrant model, which collectively projects all of your responses with one dominant philosophy. Figure II (following page) displays the four-quadrant model. I entitled it "The Animal-Rights Philosophy Index." The philosophies to respect and to defend animals' rights are plotted vertically. Items representing the philosophy to respect animals' rights carry a value of four points; defending them is worth six. So, multiply the total number of items falling under the Respect column by four, and add that product to the product of the total number of items falling under the Defend column times six. Your vertical plot is the sum of those two products: the number of Respect responses times four plus the number of Defend responses times six.

Items falling under the Ignore column carry a value of four points; and those falling under the Exploit column carry a value of six. The combined values of Ignore and Exploit responses are plotted on Figure II horizontally.

Figure II

The Animal-Rights Philosophy Index

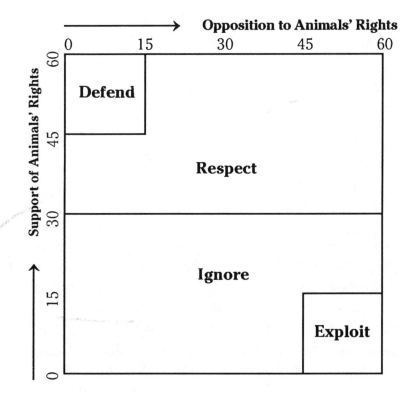

Figure III (following pages) displays the values and plot directions of the four animal-rights philosophies. Simply multiply the number of responses representing a particular philosophy by its vertical or horizontal value; do the same for each of the other three philosophies.

Figure III

Philosophy Values and Plotting Directions

Philosophy	Vertical Plot Value	Horizontal Plot Value
Exploit	0	6
Ignore	0	4
Respect	4	0
Defend	6	0

Suppose you responded to the ten situations with no Exploit responses, one Ignore response, seven Respect responses, and two Defend responses. Multiplying the seven Respect responses by four and adding that to the product of the two Defend responses times six yields a vertical plot of 40 (28 + 12)—just shy of a philosophy to defend animals' rights. The single Ignore response, when multiplied times four, provides an insignificant response of four. With these scores, this indicator of the direction of your Animal-Rights Philosophy would project your philosophy as respecting the rights of animals. The ideal style is defending animals' rights.

OTHER FOUR-QUADRANT MODELS BY THIS AUTHOR

Dr. Silverman is extensively published in professional journals and cited in academic textbooks regarding his use of four-quadrant models to measure perceptions in management. His four-quadrant "Upward Communication Model" suggests a *Formal, Passive, Active,* or *Informal* style of behavior for use with the boss by projecting the image created of the subordinate from a combination of the subordinate's credentials and experience with the boss's ambition and job security. In that model, no particular style is considered ideal.

His four-quadrant "Equal Employment Opportunity Philosophy Index" associates an individual's preferred resolution to various hypothetical situations with the extremely liberal *Benefactor* philosophy, which tends to support favorable decisions affecting protected parties to compensate for a perception of inevitable discrimination taking place elsewhere; the moderately liberal *Advocate* philosophy, which tends to side in favor of protected parties to compensate for perceived systemic discrimination already working against them; the moderately conservative *Scholar* philosophy, which tends to favor decisions against the interests of protected parties to compensate for the perception that their credentials were not likely to have been earned in accordance with established standards; or the extremely conservative *Judge* philosophy, which tends to agree with the decisions that would yield unfavorable results for protected parties to compensate for a perception of reverse discrimination taking place elsewhere. A philosophy that falls on a fine line between an *Advocate* and *Scholar* would be considered in that model to be ideal.

Chapter 11

The Animal Analogies

*T*o appreciate the implications of your perceived animal-rights philosophy, examine why a given response to a situation presented in the preceding "Animal-Rights Philosophy Index" represents a particular philosophy. Your perceptions regarding whether to defend, respect, ignore, or exploit animals' rights in a given situation may be indicative of your holding a philosophy justifying that behavior, but it may also be the result of either inhibitions contraining your free will or impulses. The next exercise I developed will reveal your actual—as distinct from perceived—animal-rights philosophy through your answers to a series of analogies.

You will be presented with a pair of words followed by four additional pairs of words. Simply choose the pair of words that best matches the relationship suggested by the first two words. For example, the relationship of man to boy is obviously more similar to that of cat and kitten than it would be to dog and cow. That simple example would be presented in the following way:

> Man : Boy ::
> 1) Dog : Cow   2) Cat : Kitten
> 3) Rat : Rabbit   4) Cat : Puppy

These Animal Analogies force word associations that will reveal your actual animal-rights philosophy. If your actual animal-rights philosophy is more progressive toward the defense of animals than your perceived philosophy, the implication is that you perceive inhibitions as constraining your free will to react spontaneously. It is very rare that a person's perceived animal-rights philosophy is more progressive than his or her actual philosophy. That could be explained by less than forthright responses to the situations plotted on "The Animal-Rights Philosophy Index."

In very rare cases, it could suggest that the person's apparent support of animals' rights is nothing more than a cover for an ulterior motive. But it is more probable that the person failed to acknowledge inhibitions constraining his or her free will. An example of such inhibitions would be insecurity brought on by a desire to conform.

For each of the following ten sets of analogies, circle the pair of words from the four alternatives that best represents the original pair. In the example provided, the alternative of "cat : kitten" best represents "man : boy."

A. Hunting : Nature ::
      1) Swimming : Water   2) Walking : Health
      3) Molesting : Children   4) Cursing : Etiquette

B. Pain : Animal ::
      1) Curfew : Teenager   2) Pain : Human
      3) Work : Bureaucrat   4) School : Child

118

C. Soul : Human ::
    1) Leather : Cow   2) Name : Pet
    3) Love : Dog   (4) Soul : Animal

D. Vivisection : Medicine ::
    1) Theft : Religion   2) Fuel : Transportation
    3) Fraud : Education   4) Sneakers : Tennis

E. Meat : Culture ::
    1) Holocaust : Germany   2) Pornography : Literature
    3) Radio : Car   (4) Prayer : Religion

F. Circus : Animal ::
    1) Game : Child   2) Cleaning : Rag
    (3) Rape : Victim   4) Cigarette : Tobacco

G. Fur : Mink ::
    (1) Skin : Human   2) Murder : Pleasure
    3) Head : Broccoli   4) Topping : Pizza

H. Cosmetics : Safety ::
    1) Chemicals : Animals   (2) Product : Experiments
    3) Simulations : Tissues 4) Natural : Pure

I. Leather : Vinyl ::
    1) Unnecessary : Adequate (2) Genuine : Imitation
    3) Cruelty : Compassion 4) Expensive : Cheap

J. Factories : Farms ::
    (1) Production : Slavery   2) Apples : Oranges
    3) Apples : Apples   4) Production : Production

Figure IV
Scoring the Animal Analogies

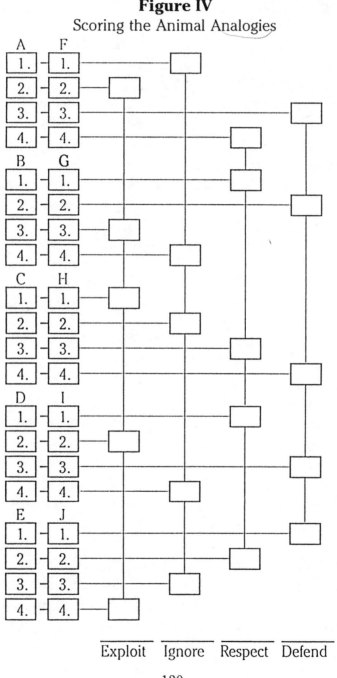

Exploit   Ignore   Respect   Defend

Now go back and underline the pair of words that provides the next best representation of the original pair of words. In the example where "cat : kitten" was the best analogy for "man : boy," the alternative of "cat : puppy" would provide the next best choice.

On Figure IV, enter five points in the box corresponding with the most representative choice selected for each item, and three points in the box corresponding to the next best representation. Then transfer the numbers to the boxes horizontally aligned to their right. Simply total the five boxes in each of the four columns formed vertically over the words Exploit, Ignore, Respect, and Defend. The philosophy with the highest point total is tentatively your actual animal-rights philosophy—tentatively because of second thoughts on the word associations that inevitably come upon reflection on their meanings. Feel free to change your responses as you reflect.

Interpreting the Analogies

The *first set* presents four different analogies between the relationship of hunting and nature. Each of the analogies typifies values for those who hold a particular animal-rights philosophy—that of exploiting, ignoring, respecting, and defending. In handling this type of question, it is necessary to determine the exact relationship between the two words for each alternative. In this case, the relationship is that hunting makes appropriate use of nature if the alternative you select is "swimming : water." That would typify the response of one who holds a philosophy of ignoring animals' rights as being the right thing to do. Walking is good for health. Thus the alternative "walking : health" suggests that hunting is good for nature.

121

That type of thinking is indicative of one who believes that exploiting animals' rights is the right thing to do. The tragic act of molesting hurts children, while the alternative of "cursing : etiquette" represents only something that is inappropriate as distinct from harmful. One who holds the philosophy of defending animals' rights would probably select the alternative "molesting : children"; the philosophy of respecting animals' rights is best represented by the alternative "cursing : etiquette."

The premise that hunting makes appropriate use of nature is presumably why, for more than fifty years, upwards of 5,000 pigeons are blown to pieces at the annual Fred Coleman Pigeon Shoot at Hegin, Pennsylvania, every Labor Day. At the 1989 "shoot," many participants wore shirts that read "Shoot Birds, Not Drugs." In 1990, some of the shirts sported slogans advocating the shooting of animals' rights advocates. And at that same shoot, one small boy tore the head off a live and uninjured pigeon, then threw it in a protestor's face.

A belief that hunting is good for nature—presumably to prevent overpopulation and starvation—is analogous to supporting human genocide as the solution for world hunger. Hunters do not hunt to help nature. Serial killer Ted Bundy randomly selected human victims as his form of recreation, just as hunters randomly select animals as their form of recreation. In the keynote address at a 1990 convention held by a group that had formed to promote the sport of hunting, a speaker was quoted by the *Washington Times* as saying, "Outdoor sports are part of our American heritage, culture, and character. Hunting keeps us in touch with nature and the elements. It is an escape from urbanization, a restatement of our individuality." The speaker also pointed out an alleged need for hunters to "harvest" animals as a means of preventing their starvation, but it was his depiction of hunting as a sport and escape from urbanization that captured the essence of why most hunters hunt: not to help nature.

A more chilling reason for hunting was offered to a reporter by a man who had just murdered a deer at the Mason Neck National Wildlife Refuge in Lorton, Virginia, during an October 1990 archery hunt. Beaming, the hunter proclaimed, "It was a thrill to see that deer drop." When pressed for a more explicit account of his reaction to having killed the deer, the hunter replied, "I can only compare that feeling to my honeymoon night when I was with my wife for the first time."

To understand why hunting is bad for nature, one need only consider that, unlike predatory animals, which select the weakest part of the wildlife population as their prey, hunters target the healthiest animals needed to keep their populations strong. As described in PETA fact sheets, hunting causes an ecological imbalance that exerts a chain reaction adversely affecting every species.

Accepting that hunting makes inappropriate use of nature acknowledges the suffering of wounded animals who die a slow and agonizing death. These wounded animals far outnumber those that hunters claim. The thrill of a hunter's chase for an animal terrorizes the entire animal kingdom, producing the same acute distress experienced by a frantically fleeing pedestrian being stalked by a mugger on a dimly lit city street. The small proportion of Americans who hunt make the majority of animals suffer.

The *second set* of analogies compares the relationship

of pain to an animal with four other analogies: curfew to a teenager, pain to a human, work to a bureaucrat, and school to a child. The first option, that of curfew to a teenager, represents something anticipated and experienced as undesirable to the subject. One who respects animals' rights would agree that an animal anticipates and experiences pain as something undesirable. Thus, the alternative "curfew : teenager" would be a typical choice of someone who holds the philosophy of respecting animals' rights.

The analogy of "pain : animal" and "pain : human" presents the most likely best representation to adherents of the philosophy of defending animals' rights. Pain is the same regardless of the species. Driving a nail into the paw of a puppy would hurt the same as driving that nail into the tender hand of a child.

Traditionally, bureaucrats view work in the manner described as Theory Y—as natural as play or rest—by Douglas McGregor, the late Sloan Professor of Management at the Massachusetts Institute of Technology. Only one who exploits animals' rights would perceive the relationship of pain to an animal with being as natural as play or rest.

One who ignores animals' rights would typically view the alternative "school : child" as the best representation of "pain : animal" under the premise that just as school is necessary, although stressful to a child, so too an animal must allegedly endure pain for its niche in society.

If you select anything other than the alternative "pain : human" as the most representative, ask yourself why.

Regardless of whether you believe a person has a soul, the *third set* of analogies presents the most definitive test of your philosophy toward animals' rights. One who holds a philosophy supporting exploitation of animals' rights would almost certainly select the alternative "leather : cow" as most representative of "soul : human." A material product such as leather would be the most important thing that person would perceive an animal to be leaving behind, as distinct from a human, whose soul is believed to be immortal.

The second alternative analogy to "soul : human" is "name : pet", which ignores the sensitivity of an animal. One who ignores animals' rights would likely select this alternative.

One who respects animal-rights issues might typically select the "love : dog" alternative out of respect for the animal's feelings even if they are perceived to be of lesser importance than a human's.

The final alternative compares "soul : human" with the analogy of a soul to an animal—the obvious choice of one who defends animals' rights. Perhaps the most vivid portrayal of an animal's soul was written, ironically, by a hunter named Corey Ford shortly before his death in 1969. His "Road to Tinkhamtown" captures the reflections on a deceased dog named Shad as the author himself faced death: "He had never married; Shad was his family. . . It was hard to believe [Shad] was gone." Ford was writing about himself in the third person, and Tinkhamtown was the place where he would experience his soul separating from his body into an immortal state. When death was imminent, Shad reappeared. Corey Ford's story ends, "Steady, boy. . . I'm coming."

It is ironic that Ford could convey such touching respect for an animal yet still depict himself as a hunter. What if some other hunters had sighted Shad as their prey?

125

What could he say to those who loved the animals he might have shot? To me, "The Road to Tinkhamtown" may be the greatest love story ever written, yet the protagonist is characterized in an illustration as toting the ultimate symbol of hate: a hunting rifle.

The *fourth set* of analogies presents the association of vivisection and medicine with the four contrasting analogies of theft and religion, fuel and transportation, fraud and education, and sneakers and tennis.

Theft is a clear violation of any religious principles. Associating what vivisection represents to medicine with that analogy is indicative of a philosophy supportive of respecting animals' rights.

The analogy of fuel and transportation represents something that is indisputably necessary. A belief that vivisection is a necessary component of medicine reflects disinterest in alternative testing methods. It reflects a blindness of, even disdain for, animals' rights.

Fraud to education represents the most extreme possible contradiction of purpose. While theft could conceivably be rationalized as necessary in certain situations, fraud cannot. Stealing to save a life is understandable; cheating to obtain an academic degree is not. An association of the relationship of vivisection to medicine with the analogy of fraud to education can be inferred as believing that vivisection contradicts the purpose of medicine and could never be justified on moral grounds under any circumstances. That is the philosophy of one who defends animals' rights.

The relationship of sneakers to tennis represents something that is helpful. A belief that vivisection is helpful to medicine represents a philosophy of ignoring

126

animals' rights.

Aside from the immorality of vivisection, its actual benefit to medicine is questionable. In the previously cited paper authored by Roy Kupsinel, M.D., for the group People for Reason in Science and Medicine, incredible differences are revealed between the effects of various drugs on animals and humans. According to Dr. Kupsinel, aspirin kills cats and penicillin kills guinea pigs; on the other hand, arsenic is safe for sheep and cyanide is safe for owls. After being thoroughly tested on animals, the tranquilizer thalidomide was found safe; of course, it produced mass birth defects and fetal deaths in humans.

The *fifth set* of analogies forces an association between the relationship of meat to culture with Holocaust to Germany, pornography to literature, radio to car, and prayer to religion.

A defender of animals' rights would consider meat to represent the most shameful product of modern society. Certainly nothing can ever be more shameful to Germany than the Holocaust. Associating meat with the ultimate crime against society is indicative of a philosophy to defend animals' rights.

The relationship of pornography to literature can be inferred as indecent, but also justified if perceived to offer socially redeeming values. One who holds to a philosophy of respecting animals' rights would associate the analogy of pornography to literature with the relationship of meat to culture.

The philosophy of ignoring animals' rights is shown in those who would associate the analogy of radio to car with meat to culture. A radio adds something positive to a car. A person who ignores animals' rights would be apt to believe that meat adds something positive to culture.

The analogy of prayer to religion represents something that is not only positive but necessary. A philosophy of exploiting animals' rights holds that meat is a necessary part of culture.

The *sixth set* of analogies forces an association of circus to animal with game to child, cleaning to rag, rape to victim, and cigarette to tobacco. The relationship of game to child is that of something natural. Holding that an animal is a natural part of a circus is a philosophy that ignores animals' rights.

To those who approve of exploiting animals' rights, the relationship of cleaning to rag best represents the analogy of circus to animal. A rag is a dispensable but necessary part of cleaning.

The relationship of rape to victim will be recognized by defenders of animals as best represented by the analogy of circus to animal. Those who adhere to a philosophy of defending animals' rights recognize the demeaning and unnatural aspects of a circus.

The less severe but negative analogy of cigarette to tobacco represents a philosophy that is respectful of animals' rights. Like a cigarette, a circus is harmful to your health—that is, if you are unfortunate enough to belong to an animal species.

A PETA fact sheet describes the confinement, coercion, and misery that result in a three-ring circus of abuse for animals: "The tricks that animals are forced to perform —bears balancing on balls, apes riding motorcycles, elephants standing on two legs—are physically uncomfortable and . . . demean the animals' dignity." Humiliation is just as painful for animals as it is for humans. Forced to spend the majority of their time in small cages and often deprived of water, the animals are forced to tolerate environments different than their natural habitats and endure pain in training.

The *seventh set* of analogies forces an association with the analogy of fur to mink with skin to human, murder to pleasure, head to broccoli, and topping to pizza.

The grotesque thought of a coat made of human skin comes to mind with the philosophy to respect animals' rights at the sight of a human wearing fur.

One whose philosophy it is to defend animals' rights would likely associate the analogy of fur to mink with the analogy of murder to pleasure—which may prompt a confrontation with the person wearing the fur.

Because the head of broccoli is widely considered to be the most important part of that vegetable, an association of fur to mink with head to broccoli suggests that an animal's pelt is his or her most important, or only important, part. That is the philosophy of one who morally supports exploiting animals.

Topping to pizza is a less extreme version of head to broccoli, because it is more customary to dispose of broccoli stems than pizza crust. Selecting the analogy of topping to pizza as that which is most closely associated with the relationship of fur to mink denotes a philosophy that ignores animals' right.

A flyer put out by the Animal Protection Institute of America brings you face to face with the sad-looking eyes of a raccoon with the following text: "Wet, freezing, in agony for hours (perhaps even days), this beautiful creature faces painful death, caught in a bone-crushing steel-jaw trap. Maybe he'll escape by chewing his own foot off, to suffer lingering torture and probably die anyway." But the most gruesome atrocities inflicted upon animals with beautiful pelt are seen on fur farms where animals such as mink are killed *en masse* with gas, electric shot, or chest-crushing asphyxiation. In the September/October 1989 issue of *PETA News,* a caretaker of a fur farm reportedly "smiled and said: 'Jewish people were killed by the Deutsch people in the small house . . . we are using the same method for mink killing.' "

The *eighth set* of analogies forces selection of the closest analogy with the relationship of cosmetics to safety from among chemicals to animals, product to experiments, simulations to tissues, and natural to pure.

A philosophy supportive of exploiting animals would lead one to choose chemicals to animals as the closest analogy on the premise that animals would be needed to test the chemicals for safety.

The analogy of product to experiments ignores animals' rights with the assumption that a product must be tested for safety.

Associating simulations to tissues with the relationship of cosmetics to safety shows respect of animals' rights through recognition of valid and reliable alternatives to animal-based research. Computer simulations and tissue cultures are just two of many meaningful alternatives to testing products on animals.

The surest safety test for cosmetics is reliance on natural and pure products that are already known to be safe. That is the safest approach for animals and the safest for human beings as well.

Another flyer from the Animal Protection Institute of America captures the agony of product testing on animals with this painful recollection of a look inside an animal laboratory: " 'I'd never heard a rabbit scream before,' cried out a heart-stricken lab worker, assigned to spray detergent powder down the throats of rabbits. 'Oh God, you have no idea!' "

The *ninth set* of alternatives compares the relationship of leather to vinyl with that of unnecessary to adequate, genuine to imitation, cruelty to compassion, and expensive to cheap.

A personal philosophy respectful of animals' rights would condition one to view leather as unnecessary and vinyl as adequate. On the other hand, one holding a philosophy supportive of exploiting animals' rights would likely view leather as genuine and vinyl as imitation.

A philosophy of defending animals' rights would enable one to see leather as a symbol of cruelty and vinyl as a symbol of compassion. One who ignores animals' rights would likely view leather as expensive and vinyl as cheap.

Cattle are slaughtered for their meat and skin; and their skin is leather. The most compelling sentiment expressed against the use of leather was uttered by an animal-rights activist to a local news correspondent during the historic March for the Animals held in Washington, D.C., on June 10, 1990. When asked why he was there marching, the activist replied, "I've been to a slaughterhouse and I can't get the animals' screaming out of my ears."

The *tenth set* of analogies compares the relationship of factories and farms to the relationships of production and slavery, apples and oranges, apples and apples, and production and production. The implications are clear.

A philosophical defender of animals' rights is likely to

equate factories with production and farms with slavery, because the animals are not voluntarily employed. A philosophy that is respectful of animals' rights would be reflected by selection of apples to oranges as most representative of factories to farms. A compassionate farmer—one who respects animals' rights—would not see any relationship between the roles of factories and farms. One who ignores animals' rights may see factories and farms in a similar role—thus the analogy of apples and apples.

Exploiting animals' rights reflects a philosophy that would tend to make one view both factories and farms in terms of production. The cited flyer published by the Farm Animal Movement shows what is wrong with factory farming: "Veal calves are torn from their mothers at birth, chained by the neck in tiny crates without bedding or light, unable to turn around . . . covered with their excrement."

Afterword

I was born Robert Stephen Silverman. With the legal help of my attorney father, Abraham George (Al) Silverman, in 1975 I petitioned the Circuit Court of Fairfax County in Virginia to legally add the name of my collie, Buddy, to mine on the day he died. Eight years earlier, a British singer named Lulu had asked the question, "How do you thank someone?" when it is time to move on, in her song—number-one song of that year—"To Sir with Love." The title of that song was most fitting for the monumental demonstration of respect I intended for Buddy.

Buddy's death came six months after the death of my companion poodle, Pompo, and two years after the horrifying death of Pompo's son, Bogie. As a child, I had experienced—without the maturity to understand—the losses of a great spitz named Stroupie, a cocker spaniel named Honey, and a dog of mixed breed named Blackie. Not a day goes by without my mentioning each of their souls in my prayers.

In 1977, I located the grand-niece of Buddy and named her Lady Pompie in honor of Pompo. Seven years later, my father died and left me his companion poodle, Cappuccino, whom I used to call "The Big Guy." The day Cappuccino died, in 1990, I again petitioned the Circuit Court of Fairfax

County—this time to give Lady Pompie the same ultimate honor I had given Buddy. (The lyrics of "Lady," a 1980 number-one song by Kenny Rogers, explain why: ". . . You're the love of my life, you're my lady.") I carried the grieving Lady Pompie through Cappuccino's funeral.

I am now named Buddy Pompie Robert Stephen Silverman. A friend told me that she thought the name B. P. Robert Stephen Silverman sounded "regal." Given what the initials B. and P. represent, I agree. This is how part of the court order, signed on October 23, 1990, by the Honorable Judge Thomas J. Middleton reads:

> . . . in honor of his loving partner, Lady Pompie, who is the love of his life, and as a tribute to his beloved companions: Cappuccino, his beloved little brother, who will forever keep the memory of his father's gentleness toward him alive; Buddy, for whom he is now named and to whom Pompie is a grand-niece; Pompo, for whom Pompie is a namesake in his honor; Bogie, whose precious life he let slip away but whose legacy remains as a son of Pompo; Blackie and Honey, whom he tragically left behind; and Stroupie, his first great friend, whom he also left behind. May God bless them and forgive him.

Buddy (collie) and Pompo
(poodle) obliterated
the myth that dogs
cannot love, as
this photo
shows.

Cappuccino was so sensitive about his size that he did not like to be
held—even in the arms of his adopted father, who found this way
to gently carry him about. (Photo on left courtesy of Olga Rohall;
photo on right courtesy of Clara Silverman)

"The story of my life is very plain to read. It starts the day you came and ends the day you leave. . . . It's the story of our times, of never letting go, and if I die today I wanted you to know" (Neil Diamond, "The Story of My Life").
To those who think dogs are void of emotion and act only on instinct, Lady Pompie was so grief-stricken at Cappuccino's funeral that I had to carry her through the procession. (Photo by Clyde Lassell)

136

Appendix A:

Animal Rights Associations

ACTIVISTS FOR PROTECTIVE ANIMAL LEGISLATION (A-PAL)
P.O. Box 11743
Costa Mesa, CA 92627
Phone: (714) 540-0583

Organized to inform the general public on legislation pertaining to animal welfare. Monitors all legislation concerning animal welfare; advises and assists lawmakers who support humane animal legislation.

ACTORS AND OTHERS FOR ANIMALS (A&O)
5510 Cahuenga Blvd.
North Hollywood, CA 91601
Phone: (818) 985-6263

Consists of individuals intending to alleviate animal suffering through direct emergency aid and pet adoption; promotes "zero pet population" growth, humane education, importance of wildlife conservation, and protection of endangered species.

AMERICAN ANTI-VIVISECTION SOCIETY (AAVS)
Noble Plaza, Suite 204
801 Old York Road
Jenkintown, PA 19046
Phone: (215) 887-0816

Opposes all types of experimentation on living animals, including poisoning, burning, freezing, electric shock, food and drink

137

deprivation, and psychological torture. Sponsors research on alternative methods. Maintains a library of 400 volumes. They are affiliated with International Association Against Painful Experiments on Animals.

AMERICAN DEFENDERS
AGAINST ANIMAL MISTREATMENT (ADAM)
P.O. Box 904
Wilmington, DE 19899

Individuals united to help protect animals from cruelty and mistreatment under the law.

AMERICAN DOG OWNERS ASSOCIATION (ADOA)
1654 Columbia Turnpike
Castleton, NY 12033
Phone: (518) 477-8469

Volunteer organization of dog owners; seeks to educate the public on responsibilities of pet ownership. Currently is challenging breed-specific laws that seek to protect the public by restricting ownership of certain dog breeds, including pit bull terriers. ADOA advocates vicious-dog laws, which apply to all "bad" dogs, as well as to owners of these so-called bad dogs.

AMERICAN FUND FOR
ALTERNATIVES TO ANIMAL RESEARCH (AFAAR)
c/o Dr. Ethel Thurston
175 West 12th Street
New York, NY 10011
Phone: (212) 989-8073

Offers grants for development of non-animal alternatives to tests currently involving animals; disseminates reports, results, and abstracts of this research to funding agencies, regulatory agencies, interested scientists, and laypersons. Seeks to demonstrate that certain experiments on living animals are harmful or unnecessary to mankind; salvages animals from painful tests; supports and provides opportunities for developing new alternatives to animal testing; exerts pressure on government agencies to allocate a greater proportion of funds for developing non-animal research. Maintains library of abstracts of medical research supported by non-animal evidence; maintains speakers' bureau with films; bestows awards. Sponsors charitable programs; offers courses. Affiliated with: International Association Against Painful Experiments on Animals.

AMERICAN SOCIETY FOR
THE PREVENTION OF CRUELTY TO ANIMALS (ASPCA)
441 East 92nd Street
New York, NY 10128
Phone: (212) 876-7700

Provides effective means for the prevention of cruelty to animals; enforces all laws for the protection of animals; promotes appreciation for, and humane treatment of, animals; maintain shelters for lost, stray, or unwanted animals; operates a veterinary hospital and a major low-cost spay/neuter clinic; conducts educational programs and disseminates animal-related information for children and adults; cares for over 130,000 animals annually.

ANIMAL LEGAL DEFENSE FUND
1363 Lincoln Avenue, #7
San Rafael, CA 94901
Phone: (415) 459-0885

Attorneys and law students who seek to promote animal rights, and protect the lives and interests of animals through the use of their legal skills. Represents people and organizations working for animal rights and welfare. Maintains an animal rights "lawyer's network" with a central listing of attorneys throughout the United States who are available for animal-related legal assistance, and a library of pleadings and decisions from litigation involving animal rights and welfare issues.

ANIMAL LIBERATION (AL)
319 West 74th Street
New York, NY 10023
Phone: (212) 874-1792

Vegetarians opposed to all animal experimentation that involes the cutting, maiming, inflicting of any pain or stress or outright killing of animals. Seeks to promote animal welfare and to educate the public on the benefits of a vegetarian diet.

ANIMAL MEDICAL CENTER (AMC)
510 East 62nd Street
New York, NY 10021
Phone: (212) 838-8100

Provides quality medical and surgical care for pets; educates veterinarians, students, and technicians on clinical research in veterinary and comparative medicine.

ANIMAL POLITICAL ACTION COMMITTEE (ANPAC)
P.O. Box 2706
Washington, DC 20013
Phone: (301) 270-1057

Individual contributors who support the election and re-election campaigns of legislators who advocate animal rights. Uses individual contributions to counteract the influence of corporate and other special interest groups that exploit animals, including companion animals, farm animals, laboratory animals, and wildlife.

ANIMAL PROTECTION INSTITUTE
OF AMERICA (API)
P.O. Box 22505
Sacramento, CA 95822
Phone: (916) 422-1921

Conducts educational and informational programs to promote humane treatment of animals. Has actively fought for preserving natural populations of whales, porpoises, harp seals and other marine mammal species, for preventing dog and cat population surplus, and for abolition of the leg-hold traps. Through a volunteer network, they distribute literature promoting humane treatment of animals to schools, clubs, the media, and the public.

ANIMAL RIGHTS INTERNATIONAL (ARI)
P.O. Box 214, Planetarium Station
New York, NY 10024
Phone (212) 873-3674

Seeks to reduce or eliminate the use of animals in testing, including toxicity testing of new chemical compounds, without compromising human safety; works to lessen the pain and suffering of food animals raised on factory farms. Encourages companies that conduct tests on animals to sponsor research into methods of testing of equal or greater accuracy that do not require the use of animals, or that use fewer animals and minimize their pain and suffering.

ANIMAL RIGHTS NETWORK (ARN)
456 Monroe Turnpike
Monroe, CT 06468
Phone: (203) 452-0446

Serves to foster greater cooperation and unity within the animal rights/welfare movement; informs the public about environmental and animal right issues including the use of animals in experimentation and animal slaughterings.

ANIMAL WELFARE INSTITUTE (AWI)
P.O. Box 3650
Washington, DC 20007
Phone: (202) 337-2332

Promotes humane treatment of animals. Primary concerns include abolishing: cruel trapping devices, destruction of whales and other endangered species, excessive confinement and deprivation of animals raised for food, and mistreatment of animals used for experiments and testing. Presents Albert Schweitzer Medal annually for outstanding contributions to animal welfare. Affiliated with: Society for Animal Protective Legislation.

ASSOCIATED HUMANE SOCIETIES (AHS)
124 Evergreen Avenue
Newark, NJ 07114
Phone (201) 824-7084

Seeks to assist both wild and domestic animals: to improve living conditions and prevent abuse. Works towards legislation supporting animal welfare. Maintains shelters for injured, abused and abandoned animals. Operates Popcorn Park-Wildlife Club. Conducts educational presentations in schools.

BEAUTY WITHOUT CRUELTY U.S.A.
175 West 12th Street
New York, NY 10011
Phone: (212) 989-8073

Opposed to the painful and destructive use of animals in the production of apparel and toiletries. Informs the public of the suffering of both wild and farmed furbearing animals, of trapped wild animals, and in those animals used for the laboratory testing of cosmetics. Sponsors fashion shows of simulated fur garments and other garments without fur to demonstrate the humane alternatives to real fur. Provides information on where to obtain cruelty-free apparel and toiletries.

BID-A-WEE HOME ASSOCIATION
410 East 38th Street
New York, NY 10016
Phone: (212) 532-6395

Humane society for the adoption of dogs and cats. Seeks to provide pet adoption services, veterinary clinic services, and burial/cremation services at pet memorial parks. Offers adult education seminars and professional training programs for specialists in the areas of animal control and protection and animal-facilitated therapy. Provides counseling in pet ownership responsibility and pet loss. Conducts community outreach programs; offers speakers' bureau. Sponsors visits to school, nursing homes, and other health-related facilities. Activities centered in New York state.

BUDDHISTS CONCERNED FOR ANIMALS (BCA)
300 Page Street
San Francisco, CA 94102
Phone: (415) 485-1495

Buddhists and other individuals concerned with society's treatment of animals. Considers one's treatment of animals as a reflection of one's spiritual life. Embraces the concerns for all animals including wildlife, farm, and laboratory animals. Urges the modification of legal minimum standards for treatment of animals in commercial, scientific, military, and agricultural practices to avoid prolonged or intense suffering. Initiates investigative and legal action in cases of animal abuse.

CANINE DEFENSE FUND (CDF)
c/o American Dog Owners Association
1654 Columbia Turnpike
Castleton, NY 12033
Phone: (518) 477-8669

Established by the American Dog Owners Association to oppose ordinances, primarily applying to pit bull terriers, that restrict pet ownership in certain U.S. communities.

CARE ABOUT THE STRAYS (CATS)
P.O. Box 474
New Albany, OH 43054
Phone: (614) 855-2494

Works to educate the public on the feeding, spaying, neutering, and care of stray animals. Conducts workshops on the care of strays and various other topics having to do with the humane treatment of animals.

COALITION TO ABOLISH
THE DRAIZE RABBIT BLINDING TESTS (CADRBT)
P.O. Box 214, Planetarium Station
New York, NY 10024
Phone: (212) 873-3674

Organizations concerned with the campaign against the 40-year-old Draize test which forces chemicals into the eyes of conscious rabbits to observe the subsequent damage. Encourages industry programs reducing the pain and the number of animals used. Conducts boycotts and demonstrations. Encourages corporate funding to develop innovative nonanimal methods. Promotes research and procedures that do not involve the use of animals; works to phase out all animal testing methods. Affiliated with: Coalition to Abolish the LD50; Coalition for Non-Violent Food.

COALITION TO ABOLISH THE LD50
P.O. Box 214, Planetarium Station
New York, NY 10024
Phone: (212) 873-3674

Composed of organizations focused on abolishing the LD50 (Lethal Dose 50%), the oldest and most universally used animal test. The LD50 measures the exact amount of any substance, including cosmetics, pesticides, and household products, that poisons or gasses to death 50% of a test group of laboratory animals. Has achieved a consensus among the U.S. scientific community, regulatory agencies, and trade associations that the classic LD50 serves no useful purpose and should therefore be abolished. The coalition seeks a federal governemntal policy against the acceptance of LD50 data, and urges the adoption of this universal standard in cooperation with the international animal rights movement. Affiliated with: Coalition to Abolish the Draize Rabbit Blinding Tests; Coalition for Non-Violent Food.

COALITION FOR DRUG-FREE HORSE RACING (CDFHR)
c/o American Horse Protection Association
1000 29th Street, N.W., Suite T100
Washington, DC 20007
Phone: (202) 965-0500

Racing professionals, animal welfare advocates, legislators, and other persons interested in the elimination of drug abuse in race horses. Intent is to educate others concerning the misuse and abuse of drugs in the horse racing industry. Conducts research and compiles statistics on drug-related racing problems; seeks elimination of "permissive medication" practices (drug-induced performance of horses with injured legs, who are unfit to race). Affiliated with: American Horse Protection Association; Humane Society of the United States. Note: CDFHR is presently inactive.

145

COALITION FOR NON-VIOLENT FOOD (CNVF)
Box 214, Planetarium Station
New York, NY 10024
Phone: (212) 873-3674

Organizations and individuals who promote reducing the pain and suffering of farm animals by advocating eating only non-violent foods. Fosters a reduction in the number of animals used for food; encourages alternatives to animal food products. Advocates refining current agribusiness methods in order to reduce the pain and distress caused to factory farm animals. Promotes vegetarianism.

COALITION TO PROTECT ANIMALS IN ENTERTAINMENT (CPAE)
P.O. Box 2448
Riverside, CA 92516
Phone: (714) 682-7872

Network of organizations interested in protecting animals in the entertainment industry. A division of United Activists for Animal Rights. Provides follow-up investigation and action on reported animal abuse cases. Fosters elimination of the profiting aspect of animal cruelty in movies, T.V. commercials, circuses, zoos, rodeos, and all areas of entertainment.

COMMITTEE TO ABOLISH SPORT HUNTING (CASH)
Box 43
White Plains, NY 10605
Phone: (914) 428-7523

Works to abolish all forms of recreational hunting through public education and lobbying. Seeks to change current governmental wildlife management programs, as CASH maintains that government policies are designed primarily to provide recreational opportunities for hunters at taxpayer expense. Runs a 60-acre refuge in the Catskill Mountains, NY; also patrols other wildlife refuge areas.

COMMITTEE FOR HUMANE LEGISLATION (CHL)
1506 19th Street, N.W., Suite 3
Washington, D.C. 20036
Phone: (202) 483-8998

Seeks to protect animals by: working toward eliminating the manufacture and use of leg-hold traps; discouraging the use of animals in experimental research and testing; halting the killing of seals with the help of the U.S. Sponsors educational arm, Friends of Animals.

CONCERN FOR HELPING ANIMALS IN ISRAEL (CHAI)
P.O. Box 3341
Alexandria, VA 22302
Phone: (703) 698-0825

Individuals and organizations interested in improving the welfare of animals in Israel. Seeks to aid the Israeli animal welfare community in the construction of animal shelters and the expansion and modernization of the few, existing shelters. Provides veterinary medical equipment and supplies; actively promotes substituting sodium pentobarbitol to replace strychnine (a painful poison) for purposes of (painless) animal euthanasia in municipal pounds. Makes humane education materials available to schoolchildren, teachers and summer camps in the U.S. and Israel. Raises funds for a mobile spay/neuter clinic. Maintains speakers' bureau.

FARM ANIMAL REFORM MOVEMENT (FARM)
P.O. Box 30654
Bethesda, MD 20824
Phone: (301) 530-1737

Devoted to eliminating the abuse of farm animals and the adverse impact of animal agriculture on human health, world hunger, environmental quality, natural resources, and national economy. Sponsors conferences to train animal rights activists in promoting public respect for animal rights. Publishes flyers promoting vegetarianism and exposing both the environmental damage and health risks created by factory farming.

FARM SANCTUARY (FS)
P.O. Box 37
Rockland, DE 19732
Phone: (302) 654-9026

Representatives working to end factory farming throughout the U.S. Seeks to eliminate abusive animal agricultural practices; provide a sanctuary for abused farm animals; educates the public on factory farming. Organizes Veal Boycott and Ban the Battery Cage campaigns to protest the abuse of veal calves and battery hens; operates traveling Farm Sanctuary Mobile which assists other animal, health and environmental groups interested in organizing such campaigns in their areas.

FELINE AND CANINE FRIENDS (FCF)
505 North Bush Street
Anaheim, CA 92805
Phone: (714) 635-7975

Provides education in the humane treatment of animals and promotes animal welfare through the prevention of cruelty. Offers free spay and neuter services when the pet owner cannot afford to pay. Operates Animobile rescue vans. Conducts educational programs in schools and for youth organizations and special interest groups.

FRIENDS OF ANIMALS (FOA)
Box 1244
Norwalk, CT 06856
Phone: (203) 866-5223

Works to reduce the number of stray animals by educating pet owners to prevent the birth of unwanted pets. Offers low-cost spay/neuter programs and assists animal shelters within the program. Actively boycotts furs. Fights for banning steel jaw leg-hold traps, protecting U.S. seals from slaughter, and eliminating wildlife destruction.

FUND FOR ANIMALS
200 West 57th Street
New York, NY 10019
Phone: (212) 246-2096

Works to protect wildlife and fight cruelty to animals, both domestic and wild, by means of legal aciton, direct activism, public education, and lobbying. Motto is "We Speak for Those Who Can't"; bumper stickers and buttons reflect theme, "Animals Have Rights, Too." Publicizes and influences public opinion on environmental and animal issues through books, press releases, articles, meetings, and special events. Has exposed the cruelty of bullfighting, the clubbing of baby seals, use of the leg-hold trap, and sport hunting. Initiates national debates on issues such as laboratory animals, greyhound racing, and dog fighting. Has succeeded in placing over 170 animal species on the endangered species list. Owns and operates Black Beauty Farm in Texas for homeless and abused horses and the Animal Trust Sanctuary in Ramona, CA, a shelter for dogs, cats, and small wild animals.

HUMANE FARMING ASSOCIATION (HFA)
1550 California Street
San Francisco, CA 94109
Phone: (415) 485-1495

Produces educational materials on what the association believes are inhumane practices currently used in animal breeding and animal farming—including factory farming, genetic engineering, and slaughterhouses. Organizes national demonstrations to advocate veal boycotts; has introduced legislation outlawing the veal crate.

HUMANE SOCIETY OF THE UNITED STATES (HSUS)
2100 L Street, N.W.
Washington, D.C. 20037
Phone: (202) 452-1100

Works to promote "the humane treatment of animals and to instill compassion in mankind." Fosters a humane ethic and philosophy through educational, legislative, investigative, and legal activities. Goals include: reducing the overbreeding of cats and dogs; promoting responsible pet care; eliminating cruelty in hunting and trapping; exposing and eliminating the plight of animals in research; eliminating the abuse of animals in entertainment; correcting inhumane conditions for animals in zoos and other exhibits; stoppng cruelty in the raising, handling, and transporting of animals used for food.

HUMANS AGAINST RABBIT EXPLOITATION (HARE)
P.O. Box 1553
Williamsport, PA 17703
Phone: (717) 322-3252

International coalition of animal protection groups. Opposes all forms of exploitation of rabbits, with particular focus on the "factory farming" of rabbits by the rabbit breeding industry.

Seeks to foil the rabbit breeding industry through a number of means: education, legislation, economic boycott, and protest. Stages protests at conferences on rabbit breeding and usage. Opposes promotion of rabbit as a meat source; encourages avoidance of all products of the rabbit industry and of boycotts against stores and restaurants that sell rabbit meat and against universities offering rabbit breeding courses. Affiliated with: Trans-Species Unlimited.

IN DEFENSE OF ANIMALS (IDA)
21 Tamal Vista Blvd.
Corte Madera, CA 94925
Phone: (415) 924-4454

Individuals interested in taking direct action to protect animals from "cruel treatment in the name of science." Conducts demonstrations and protests at laboratories conducting experiments on live animals.

INTERNATIONAL ANIMAL RIGHTS ALLIANCE (IARA)
P.O. Box 1836 GMF
Boston, MA 02205
Phone: (617) 734-4068

Individuals concerned about environmental issues, responsibile use of energy, animal rights and world hunger who believe the commercial production of meat causes unwarranted suffering to animals; encourages economic boycott of institutions with high meat consumption such as McDonald's. Sponsors the Boycott Burger King Coalition.

INTERNATIONAL DEFENDERS OF ANIMALS (IDA)
Box 175
San Martin, CA 95046
Phone: (408) 778-5577

Individuals interested in animal welfare and in the abolition of vivisection. Activities include: humane education; birth control of domestic pets; pet adoption service; care for sick, injured, or homeless animals; investigation of cases of cruelty to animals. Promotes general interest in birds and other animals. Bestows awards.

INTERNATIONAL FUND FOR
ANIMAL WELFARE (IFAW)
P.O. Box 193
Varmouth Port, MA 02675
Phone: (617) 362-4944

Purposes are to protect animal species; prevent cruelty to animals; mitigate animal suffering; promote cooperation among national and international organizations having these same purposes.

INTERNATIONAL NETWORK
FOR RELIGION AND ANIMALS (INRA)
P.O. Box 1335
North Wales, PA 19454
Phone: (215) 699-6067

Network that tries to influence both Western and Eastern religious organizations toward changing the attitudes of their congregations towards animals. It tries to use religious principles to influence humanity's attitude toward animals. Issues of concern include use of animals and animal products as food, clothing, animals in entertainment and the treatment of experimental laboratory animals.

INTERNATIONAL PRIMATE PROTECTION LEAGUE (IPPL)
P.O. Box 766
Summerville, SC 29484
Phone: (803) 871-2280

Zoologists, primate field workers, anthropologists, and interested individuals; humane societies and animal welfare organizations. Purpose is to conserve and protect nonhuman primates. Works to protect primate habitat, reduce primate trade, and detect smuggling of primates; and also works to improve conditions of zoo and laboratory primates. Monitors international trade in primates.

INTERNATIONAL SOCIETY FOR ANIMAL RIGHTS (ISAR)
421 South State Street
Clarks Summit, PA 18411
Phone: (717) 586-2200

Seeks to prevent exploitation and abuse in animals; provides and distributes literature on subjects of animal abuse and exploitation; circulates a documentary film collection to schools and colleges throughout the U.S.; sponsors seminars and organizes demonstrations.

MILLENNIUM GUILD (MG)
40 Central Park South
New York, NY 10019
Phone: (212) 755-2559

Vegetarians who believe that the millennium (a period of universal peace) will arrive only when man "evolves a true sense of the right of all races, human and sub-human," and that all creatures have a right to life and should be protected by human beings. Opposes the killing of animals for food and use of animals in medical research.

MORRIS ANIMAL FOUNDATION (MAF)
45 Inverness Drive, E.
Englewood, CO 80112
Phone: (303) 790-2345

Objective is to fund studies into the diseases and health problems of companion and zoo animals in order to find ways to cure them and maintain their health. Sponsors Ride for Research, Dog-A-Thon and animal health seminars.

NATIONAL ALLIANCE FOR ANIMAL LEGISLATION
(The Alliance)
P.O. Box 75116
Washington, DC 20013
Phone: (703) 684-0654

Seeks to develop a network of individuals to promote legislation protecting animals and their environment and teach the public how to use the legislative process to establish laws protecting animals. Lobbies on Capitol Hill; sponsors training conferences and workshops nationwide. Sells publications on human treatment of animals.

NATIONAL ANIMAL CONTROL ASSOCIATION (NACA)
P.O. Box 321
Indianola, WA 98342
Phone: (206) 297-3293

Animal shelters, humane societies, public health and safety agencies, corporations, and individuals. Works to educate and train personnel in the animal care and control professions. Seeks to teach the public responsible pet ownership.

NATIONAL ANTI-VIVISECTION SOCIETY (NAVS)
53 West Jackson, Suite 1550
Chicago, IL 60604
Phone: (312) 427-6065

Persons interested in animal welfare. Conducts educational program to acquaint the public with the "evils of vivisection of animals" and to teach the methods and means of combatting vivisection.

NATIONAL ASSOCIATION FOR THE ADVANCEMENT OF HUMANE EDUCATION (NAAHE)
c/o Humane Society of the U.S.
P.O. Box 362
East Haddam, CT 06423
Phone: (203) 434-8666

Seeks to improve humane education programs nationally by providing leadership, practical ideas, and materials. Provides consultation for local school systems, educations organizations, and humane societies interested in incorporating humane concepts into their educational master plan.

NATIONAL CAT PROTECTION SOCIETY (NCPS)
1528 West 17th Street
Long Beach, CA 90813
Phone: (213) 436-3162

Organized to control cat breeding, institute a program of euthanasia for homeless cats, promote a human education program to enlighten the American public about needs for cat protection; form a group of trained humane officers to investigate cases of cruelty and neglect; open and operate a cat shelter.

NATIONAL CONGRESS OF
ANIMAL TRAINERS AND BREEDERS (NCATB)
Route 1, Box 32H
23675 West Chardon Road
Grayslake, IL 60030
Phone: (312) 546-0717

Seeks to prevent the extinction of rare animals by opposing endangered species laws and government regulations that prohibit the sale or trade of such animals and thus prevent breeding. Monitors government activities regarding animal legislation; testifies at government hearings on pending legislation.

NATIONAL DOG REGISTRY (NDR)
Box 116
Woodstock, NY 12498
Phone: (914) 679-2355

Seeks to reduce the traffic in stolen dogs and expedite the identification of lost, strayed, injured, or dead dogs. Since dogs are difficult to identify without a dog tag—whether lost or removed—the registry encourages owners to have an identification number tattooed on the right hind leg of their pet as permanent identification and, for a small fee, to register this number with the NDR. NDR is recognized as a center for identification of lost dogs and is used regularly by law enforcement agencies, humane societies, dog handlers and others for obtaining information on lost or unidentified animals.

NATIONAL HUMANE EDUCATION SOCIETY (NHES)
211 Gibson Street, N.W., Suite 104
Leesburg, VA 22075
Phone: (703) 777-8319

Purposes are to fight for the prevention of cruelty to animals in any form including hunting and fur trapping; promote enlightened, humane behavior to enhance, rather than harm, the lives of animals; rescue homeless cats and dogs and provide permanent care for them; oppose poisoning of wildlife; protect and conserve wildlife; promote kindness and compassion toward animals; advance programs for humane sterilization of animals to reduce overpopulation.

PEOPLE FOR THE ETHICAL TREATMENT OF ANIMALS
(PETA)
Box 42516
Washington, DC 20015
Phone: (301) 770-7444

Educational and activist group that opposes all forms of animal exploitation. Seeds to educate the public against speciesism and human chauvinist attitudes toward animals through documentary films, slides, and pictures of current conditions in slaughterhouses and experimentation laboratories. Conducts three major institutionalized cruelty issues; the exploitation and abuse of animals in experimentation, the manufacturing of fur apparel, and slaughtering for human consumption.

PSYCHOLOGISTS FOR THE
ETHICAL TREATMENT OF ANIMALS (PsyETA)
P.O. Box 87
New Gloucester, ME 04260
Phone: (207) 926-4817

Seeks to ensure proper treatment of animals used in psychological research and education. Urges revision of curricula to include ethical issues in the treatment of animals. Works to establish procedures that would reduce the number of animals used in experiments; encourages creation of institutional policy to regulate animal use and possible abuse.

RETIRED GREYHOUNDS AS PETS (REGAP)
1306 Bunker Hill Road
Mooresville, IN 46158
Phone: (317) 996-2154

Seeks to find homes for retired greyhounds as well as greyhounds that have not had successful racing careers. Promotes
retired greyhounds as loving, beautiful pets.

SCIENTISTS CENTER FOR ANIMAL WELFARE (SCAW)
4805 St. Elmo Avenue
Bethesda, MD 20814
Phone: (301) 654-6390

Supports justifiable research on animals, but believes that humane concern for animals should be incorporated into all areas
of science. Provides forum for the discussion of public account-
ability, public policy, and the scientist's responsibilities
regarding standards of animal care and use; promotes ethical
discourse on biomedical, agricultural, and wildlife research
procedures.

SCIENTISTS' GROUP FOR
REFORM OF ANIMAL EXPERIMENTATION (SGRAE)
147-01 Third Avenue
Whitestone, NY 11357
Phone: (718) 767-8670

Composed of physicians, dentists, and veterinarians, research
scientists and students. Promotes a humane approach to animal
experimentation in biological research, testing, and education;
seeks to prevent cruel and unethical procedures. Encourages
the development and use of alternatives to animal experimentation. Opposes pound seizure of animals for experimentation;
believes that all experimental animals should be purpose-bred.
Encourages experimenters to replace use of animals whenever

possible, reduce the number of animals used, and refine the procedures used in order to minimize stress on the animal.

SIMIAN SOCIETY OF AMERICA (SSA)
3625 Watson Road
St. Louis, MO 63109
Phone: (314) 647-6218

Zoo staff members, veterinarians, professional primatologists, humane workers, pet dealers, and others who own or handle monkeys. Seeks to promote better husbandry and general conditions for monkeys living in captivity. Exchanges information on the biological and psychological needs of monkeys in captivity and on humane and conservation activities.

SOCIETY AGAINST VIVISECTION (SAV)
P.O. Box 10206
Costa Mesa, CA 92627
Phone: (714) 540-0583

Grass-roots organization seeking to abolish vivisection. Subsidizes pet spaying and neutering. Provides animal rescue services.

SOCIETY FOR ANIMAL PROTECTIVE LEGISLATION (SAPL)
P.O. Box 3719, Georgetown Station
Washington, DC 20007
Phone: (202) 337-2334

Purpose is to protect animals through legislation. Prepares information for use by members of Congress and their staffs. Disseminates information, through correspondence, to persons interested in progress of proposed state and federal legislation for the protection of animals.

STUDENT ACTION CORPS FOR ANIMALS (SACA)
P.O. Box 15588
Washington, DC 20003
Phone: (202) 543-8983

Primarily high school and college students. Seeks to encourage youth participation in the animal rights movement and to enhance awareness of animal rights issues. Aids in organization of local groups; serves as national network and clearinghouse and as an advocacy and counseling group.

TRANS-SPECIES UNLIMITED (TSU)
P.O. Box 1553
Williamsport, PA 17703
Phone: (717) 322-3252

Aims to develop a comprehensive educational program; expose specific cases of animal abuse and seek redress through persuasive and legal means; protest, nonviolently, against abuse of animals; foster cooperation within the rights movement; promote awareness of the natural relationship between human and animal liberation.

UNEXPECTED WILDLIFE REFUGE (UWR)
Unexpected Road
P.O. Box 765
Newsfield, NJ 08344
Phone: (609) 697-3541

Promotes education, especially of children, concerning the humane treatment of animals; protection of animals in the refuge; study of wildlife in the field; writing of observations for publication. Operates a 400-acre wildlife refuge, plants trees and crops for the animals, and guides small groups of visitors.

UNITED ACTION FOR ANIMALS (UAA)
205 East 42nd Street; Room 1923
New York, NY 10017
Phone: (212) 983-5315

Promotes research using modern, sophisticated methods in place of live animals. These include the use of tissue and organ culture, isolated organs, computer simulation, mathematical modeling and mechanical models such as those used in car crash tests. Seeks legislation to provide federal funding of existing alternatives and the development of more alternatives.

UNITED ACTIVISTS FOR ANIMAL RIGHTS (UAAR)
P.O. Box 2448
Riverside, CA 92516
Phone: (714) 682-7872

Opposes animal cruelty and exploitation. Seeks to abolish the fur industry, vivisection, and factory farming, and curb pet over-population. Works for the passage of animal rights legislation.

UNITED HUMANITARIANS (UH)
P.O. Box 14587
Philadelphia, PA 19115
Phone: (215) 750-0171

Establishes humane animal control through mass spaying and neutering of pets and the replacement of the present licensing system with a permit system placing complete responsibility on owners who would be cited for violations rather than impounding and killing pets found at large.

VIVISECTION INVESTIGATION LEAGUE (VIL)
40 West 59th Street
New York, NY 10019
Phone: (212) 752-5822

Protests laboratory experiments on live animlas, usually performed without anesthesia. Currently opposes the LD 50 test. Offers "Last Post" havens for cats and dogs whose owners have died, or have gone into nursing homes.

The above appendix has been compiled from *The Encyclopedia of Associations, 1991,* 24th ed., Vol. 1, Deborah M. Burek, Karen E. Koek, and Annette Novallo, eds. Copyright © 1959, 1961, 1964, 1968, 1970, 1972, 1973, 1975, 1976, 1977, 1978, 1979, 1980, 1981, 1982, 1983, 1984, 1985, 1986, 1987, 1988, 1989, 1990 by Gale Research, Inc. Reproduced by permission of the publisher.

Only selected organizations appearing under the "Animal Welfare" section in *The Encyclopedia of Associations* have been included in the foregoing list. Inclusion of a particular group does not constitute an endorsement on the author's part of its policies or even recognition of its authenticity. Nor does non-selection imply anything negative; there are many reputable animal associations that do not appear in *The Encyclopedia of Associations* that would otherwise have appeared in this listing, and there are some listed here that would likely *not* have been listed, had more information been available about them or their activities. Less than one-third of the organizations listed were responsive to my inquiries. So, a proviso is offered that you should exercise your own careful judgment before providing any of them with financial support.

For a list of organizations that, on the other hand, fund animal research/vivisection or for a list of pro-hunting organizations, the reader may write People for the Ethical Treatment of Animals, P.O. Box 42516, Washington, DC 20015, or this author through S.P.I. Books / Shapolsky Publishers, 136 West 22nd St., New York, NY 10011.

Appendix B:

How to Select a Charitable Organization to Support and to Include in Your Will

A charitable organization you should support is one that uses its resources to further a cause in which you believe. If your intent is to benefit the cause of animals' rights, you should not contribute to the various funds that have charters to search for cures of diseases for which they are typically named, because that money is likely to be used to sponsor animal research. Even if you contribute to an animal welfare organization, you cannot be certain, without specifically asking, whether it condones vivisection or hunting under certain circumstances. You also need to know how much money it has, how much it spends, and how much goes to overhead expenses—expenses that may include higher salaries among those who administer the fund than you might anticipate.

Selecting which charitable organizations to include in your will is a much more pressing issue. You never know how much time you have to write it. A growing number of people never marry or cohabit; and there is a trend among many who do marry or cohabit not to have children. Those who do marry or cohabit today face a high probability of divorce and, depending upon their respective ages, variable chances of surviving their partners' deaths. It is safe to infer from these sociological demographics that there is an increasing probability for a person to be unmarried and childless at death. That places enormous importance on your selection of a favorite charity, because it is to your favorite charity that you are most apt to bequeath your worldly possessions if you are among those who die alone. Your worldly possessions are the product of your entire life's work and your inheritance. What a pity it would be to put them to work against every principle on which you stand.

Most people are not surprised that human health organizations sponsor animal research; but, it usually does not independently occur to them. What surprises most people is the number of organizations represented as being supportive of animals' rights but which are actually supportive of animal experiments and hunting, and the number of organizations that do promote animals' rights, but only to the extent that their work is intended to make animal experiments and hunting less painful under the premise that they are either sometimes necessary or inevitable.

The most important consideration in selecting an animal-rights charity is not what your philosophy will tolerate about the organization but what the organization tolerates being done to animals. In addition to reading a charitable organization's written policy statements on specific issues, you need to know if it has sufficient assets to operate after the departure of its current operating officers. An organization with large total assets is apt to survive longer than one with total assets that are comparatively small; and the more it has available in its budget to spend, the less likely it is to fold. Much has been written about the proportions of budgets in charitable organizations that are devoted to programs and the proportions that are devoted to overhead. The most controversial issue is that of pay.

The top salaries paid by these organizations range from exceedingly low to that which is paid executives in major corporations. On one hand, organizations that do not compensate top officers adequately may find difficulty in finding suitable replacements when the current officers depart. On the other hand, the high salaries may be misleading to contributors who simply would not anticpate the organization paying salaries that high.

To help you select which charitable organizations to support and which to include in your will, this book provides listings courtesy of *The Animals' Agenda* editorial staff of the money spent, assets, and top salaries paid by charities with varying positions on animals' rights, but to which many people concerned about animals contribute.

In keeping with the spirit of disclosure, it is only fair that I reveal the terms of my publishing contract; because I too am making money in the name of animals' rights. I received $20 at the time I signed the contract and will receive an additional advance of $180 upon publication. For a paperback edition, I will receive 8 percent of the retail price on the first 25 thousand copies sold; 9 percent on the next 75 thousand; and 10 percent on all further copies sold. For a hardcover edition, I will receive 10 percent of the retail price on the first 20,000 copies sold; 12.5 percent on the next 20,000; and 15 percent on all further.

Appendix C:

How Animal Organizations Spend Their Money

*T*he *Animals' Agenda* compiled the following tables from IRS Form 990 filings for fiscal year 1989 and published an abridged version in its April 1991 issue.

Table No. 1 lists some of the most visible animal protection groups in order of the size of their 1989 budgets, along with selected other groups whose focus is on habitat. The habitat-oriented groups are included because they also receive substantial donations from people whose intent is to help wildlife. Footnotes quote from their written policies on hunting and provide further information on selected animal protection groups as well. Table No. 1 also shows the total budget of each group, how much is spent on programs, and how much is spent on maintaining the organization; e.g., on fundraising, office expenses, and salaries. According to *The Animals' Agenda*, the vast majority of groups whose direct-mail funding appeals include educational and public advocacy materials reported all of their expenses under fundraising and none of their expenses under program services. Additional footnotes identify groups whose budget breakdown does not conform with the majority of those listed, according to Kim Bartlett and Merritt Clifton of *The Animals' Agenda*.

Table No. 2 lists the animal protection groups only, in order of their total assets. Fixed assets include buildings, usually office space and/or animal shelters. In several cases the total worth of a group is somewhat misleading. Frequently the value of the land beneath an office or shelter has appreciated due to surrounding development, while cash income has grown at a slower pace. Some critics argue that groups in this position should sell their present facilities, relocate to cheaper areas, and spend the savings on new programs to help animals. But Kim Bartlett and Merritt Clifton present a convincing argument that this strategy probably wouldn't work for most such groups, because all the property in the districts they serve is expensive and the cost of building animal care facilities at a new site would exceed the return from selling the old facilities—which new owners would want to demolish. In other cases, generally involving small groups, liquid assets (cash and securities) appear high relative to budget when the groups are, in fact, struggling to make expenses. An example is Farm Sanctuary, whose 1989 cash assets included substantial pending payments on the farm that has become the group's headquarters.

Table No. 3 provides the compensation of the five highest-paid staffers of each animal protection group and identification of groups with directors who are not compensated. Footnotes are provided where individuals are paid through special arrangements reported in *The Animals' Agenda,* or where other circumstances seem to require further explanation. Salaries are associated only with position titles. All names have been deleted.

TABLE 1

ORGANIZATION	1989 BUDGET	PROGRAMS		OVERHEAD	
The Nature Conservancy	$156,100,000	$115,514,000	74%	$40,586,000	26%
National Wildlife Federation[1]	$ 87,200,000	$ 74,992,000	86%	$12,208,000	14%
Ducks Unlimited[2]	$ 67,400,000	$ 51,898,000	77%	$19,546,000	23%
Greenpeace U.S.A.	$ 50,200,000	$ 36,646,000	73%	$13,554,000	27%
World Wildlife Fund[3]	$ 41,675,073	$ 34,433,695	83%	$ 7,241,378	17%
Sierra Club[4]	$ 35,200,000	$ 23,936,000	68%	$11,264,000	32%
National Audubon Society[5]	$ 35,000,000	$ 24,500,000	70%	$10,500,000	30%
North Shore Animal League	$ 19,620,369	$ 11,699,655	60%	$ 7,920,714	40%
Massachusetts SPCA	$ 17,657,626	$ 13,706,959	78%	$ 3,950,667	22%
The Wilderness Society[6]	$ 17,300,000	$ 12,975,000	75%	$ 4,325,000	25%
American SPCA	$ 16,487,294	$ 10,918,408	66%	$ 5,568,886	34%
Humane Society of the U.S.[7]	$ 13,560,523	$ 11,125,666	82%	$ 2,434,857	18%
Sierra Club Legal Def. Fund	$ 6,700,000	$ 4,690,000	70%	$ 2,010,000	30%
PETA	$ 6,522,457	$ 4,939,540	76%	$ 1,582,917	24%
The Conservation Foundation	$ 5,605,129	$ 4,885,621	88%	$ 719,508	12%
Doris Day Animal League[8]	$ 4,737,524	$ 2,665,330	56%	$ 2,072,164	44%
Conservation International	$ 4,600,000	$ 3,910,000	85%	$ 690,000	15%
Defenders of Wildlife	$ 4,353,853	$ 3,154,650	73%	$ 1,199,203	27%
IFAW[8]	$ 4,165,313	$ 2,880,601	69%	$ 1,284,712	31%
Friends of Animals	$ 4,101,444	$ 3,447,351	84%	$ 654,093	16%
African Wildlife Foundation	$ 3,300,000	$ 2,706,000	82%	$ 594,000	18%
American Humane Assn.[9]	$ 3,231,067	$ 2,565,589	79%	$ 665,478	21%
Friends of the Earth	$ 3,100,000	$ 2,511,000	81%	$ 589,000	19%
Animal Protection Institute	$ 2,656,640	$ 1,883,379	71%	$ 773,261	29%
Connecticut Humane Society	$ 2,333,142	$ 1,999,062	87%	$ 334,080	13%
Natl. Humane Education Soc.	$ 2,236,871	$ 1,606,501	72%	$ 630,370	28%
American Rivers	$ 1,500,000	$ 1,110,000	74%	$ 394,000	26%
New Eng. Anti-Viv. Society	$ 1,472,459	$ 1,219,243	83%	$ 253,216	17%
Natl. Anti-Vivisection Soc.	$ 1,444,660	$ 977,478	68%	$ 464,182	32%
Adopt-A-Pet, Inc.[10]	$ 1,284,826	$ 489,912	38%	$ 794,914	62%
The Fund for Animals	$ 1,214,788	$ 767,586	63%	$ 447,202	37%
Earth Island Institute	$ 1,100,000	$ 869,000	79%	$ 231,000	21%
American Anti-Viv. Society	$ 984,915	$ 767,360	78%	$ 217,555	22%
Animal Legal Defense Fund	$ 972,899	$ 663,137	68%	$ 309,762	32%
The Animals' Voice[11]	$ 957,937	$ 641,319	67%	$ 316,618	33%
Physicians Com. for Resp. Med.	$ 897,401	$ 602,605	67%	$ 294,796	33%
Rainforest Action Network	$ 876,000	$ 613,200	70%	$ 262,800	30%

168

TABLE 1 (continued)

ORGANIZATION	1989 BUDGET	PROGRAMS		OVERHEAD	
Rainforest Alliance	$ 750,000	$ 532,500	71%	$ 217,500	29%
United Action for Animals[12]	$ 729,152	$ 679,250	93%	$ 49,902	7%
In Defense of Animals	$ 654,803	$ 568,774	87%	$ 86,029	13%
Humane Farming Assn.	$ 608,961	$ 473,622	78%	$ 135,339	22%
The ANIMALS' AGENDA[13]	$ 595,513	$ 424,092	71%	$ 171,421	29%
United Animal Nations	$ 590,404	$ 443,143	75%	$ 147,261	25%
Defenders of Animal Rights[8]	$ 584,338	$ 468,420	80%	$ 115,918	20%
Intl. Soc. for Animal Rights	$ 551,400	$ 373,297	68%	$ 178,103	32%
WLFA[14]	$ 523,633	$ 461,380	88%	$ 62,253	12%
Sea Shepherd Conserv. Soc.	$ 498,650	$ 413,879	83%	$ 84,771	17%
Animal Welfare Institute	$ 467,969	$ 368,374	79%	$ 99,595	21%
Trans-Species Unlimited[15]	$ 420,854	$ 366,175	87%	$ 54,679	13%
Primarily Primates[16]	$ 267,539	$ 155,676	58%	$ 111,863	42%
Assn. of Vets for Animal Rts.	$ 263,995	$ 219,339	83%	$ 44,656	17%
Intl. Primate Prot. League	$ 255,582	$ 180,390	71%	$ 75,192	29%
Earth First!	$ 212,084	$ 171,788	81%	$ 40,296	19%
FARM	$ 119,140	$ 96,817	81%	$ 20,756	19%
Farm Sanctuary	$ 92,593	$ 75,559	82%	$ 17,034	18%
PsyETA	$ 27,903	$ 17,295	62%	$ 10,608	38%

NOTES

1. An undated form letter signed by the President of the National Wildlife Federation (NWF) states: "Hunting, fishing, and trapping are but three of the human activities associated with wildlife. The NWF supports them as legitimate activities when carried out in accordance with regulations established by professionally trained wildlife managers."

2. An undated form letter signed by the New York State Chairman of Ducks Unlimited thanks members for "continued support of Ducks Unlimited and considering our involvement to the betterment of...waterfowl hunting."

3. An undated letter signed by the Public Information Director of the World Wildlife Fund states that "World Wildlife Fund does not support hunting and trapping, but neither do we universally condemn the practice."

4. The official Sierra Club policy paper on wildlife states: "Within both modified and natural ecosystems, the Sierra Club believes that acceptable management techniques include...regulated periodic hunting and fishing....(and) captive breeding of wildlife as a means of providing animals for biological and medical research."

5. A 1991 form letter signed by the Vice President of the National Audubon Society states that "Unless the population of a species listed by law as 'game' is threatened, we do not actively oppose hunting these species."

6. An undated form letter signed by a membership assistant at the Wilderness Society states: "Where hunting has been determined to be compatible with the purpose of a public land conservation unit, we consider hunting a legitimate recreational or subsistence activity."

7. In statements of policy dated May 1984, the Humane Society of the United States expressed general opposition to the use of animals in biomedical research and hunting—but with allowances that it "recognizes that benefit for both animals and mankind has been achieved through some scientific research and testing on animals"; "that the welfare and responsible management of animals may, on occasion, necessitate the killing of wildlife"; and "that the legitimate needs for human subsistence may necessitate the killing of wildlife."

8. These organizations were reported in *The Animals' Agenda* to have "counted the costs of mailing educational and public advocacy materials that included appeals for donations as program expenses, rather than as part of fundraising."—which yields a smaller overhead percentage than would have resulted with the same method of accounting that most of the other groups apparently applied.

9. The November 1990 issue of *BBC Wildlife* reported that famed television personality and animal-rights activist Bob Barker was sued for defamation by the American Humane Association for allegations regarding that group's performance at protecting animals used in motion pictures. *The Animals' Agenda* reported that "the American Humane Association program budget included $1,683,879 spent on animal protection, and $881,710 spent on child protection."

10. In the comprehensive listings compiled by *The Animals' Agenda* of financial information on animal charities, Adopt-A-Pet is reported to allegedly be "one of seven charities promoted by (a corporation) that were collectively fined $2.1 million in January 1991" for fundraising violations during 1988–1989, with additional charges pending. The group is also known as National Animal Protection Fund.

11. The corporate name is Compassion for Animals Foundation.

12. The group United Action for Animals was reported in *The Animals' Agenda* to have achieved this unusually high ratio of program expenses to overhead by incurring a deficit for the fiscal year of $541,693—amounting to 36 percent of the group's total assets at the beginning of the year.

13. The corporate name is Animal Rights Network, Inc.

14. A flier put out by the Wildlife Legislative Fund of America (WLFA) identifies itself as "a non-profit organization which protects the heritage of American sportsmen to hunt, fish and trap, and protects scientific wildlife management practices. WLFA provides legislative lobbying and legal defense services to advance sportsmen's rights."

15. Trans-Species Unlimited is now known as Animal Rights Mobilization!

16. Primarily Primates was reported in *The Animals' Agenda* to have a skewed ratio of program costs to overhead because of the labor-intensive nature of taking care of more than 300 primates and 150 birds.

TABLE 2

ORGANIZATION	TOTAL ASSETS	FIXED ASSETS	CASH/ SECURITIES
Massachusetts SPCA	$62,535,314	$15,610,084	$44,522,717
North Shore Animal League	$51,207,727	$ 2,632,691	$44,970,159
American SPCA	$39,596,797	$ 3,272,935	$28,642,980
World Wildlife Fund	$34,302,542	$ 1,414,242	$25,984,177
Humane Society of the U.S.	$22,897,352	$ 2,572,831	$18,598,727

TABLE 2 (continued)

ORGANIZATION	TOTAL ASSETS	FIXED ASSETS	CASH/ SECURITIES
Connecticut Humane Society	$16,937,571	$ 1,427,659	$15,371,960
New Eng. Anti-Viv. Society	$ 8,501,220	$ 754,914	$ 7,566,701
The Conservation Foundation	$ 6,990,939	$ 437,080	$ 5,410,932
American Anti-Viv. Society	$ 5,696,336	$ 39,332	$ 5,535,539
American Humane Assn.[1]	$ 5,271,334	$ 2,217,702	$ 2,465,400
Friends of Animals	$ 2,997,911	$ 123,357	$ 2,681,130
The Fund for Animals	$ 2,393,866	$ 662,955	$ 1,695,796
Intl. Fund for Animal Welfare	$ 2,381,829	$ 1,771,078	$ 220,662
Natl. Anti-Vivisection Soc.	$ 2,319,138	$ 41,947	$ 2,162,077
Defenders of Wildlife	$ 2,120,646	$ 355,919	$ 1,587,904
PETA	$ 1,907,444	$ 658,143	$ 49,662
Humane Farming Assn.	$ 1,401,949	$ 31,866	$ 1,386,751
United Action for Animals	$ 976,561	$ 58,074	$ 749,226
Adopt-A-Pet, Inc.	$ 491,321	$ 120,778	$ 101,840
Intl. Soc. for Animal Rights	$ 452,099	$ 166,137	$ 238,699
Primarily Primates	$ 440,128	$ 367,925	$ 77,048
Natl. Humane Education Soc.	$ 428,968	$ 343,179	$ 62,706
Animal Protection Institute	$ 302,089	$ 60,765	$ 143,970
Intl. Primate Prot. League	$ 294,286	$ 199,068	$ 95,218
Doris Day Animal League	$ 280,736	$ 9,290	$ 235,712
Farm Sanctuary	$ 192,898	$ 80,676	$ 77,224
The Animals' Voice	$ 160,668	$ 97,894	$ 62,774
PCRM	$ 109,900	$ 34,976	$ 14,696
Assn. of Vets for Animal Rts.	$ 99,408	$ 7,853	$ 91,005
Com. for Humane Legislation	$ 83,751	$ 4,981	$ 78,770
Animal Legal Defense Fund	$ 82,599	$ 16,410	$ 44,469
Trans-Species Unlimited	$ 75,344	$ 19,538	$ 50,071
Animal Welfare Institute	$ 68,713	$ 17,984	$ 49,358
In Defense of Animals	$ 58,836	(none claimed)	$ 56,915
PsyETA	$ 56,333	$ 13,000	$ 43,333
FARM	$ 25,668	(none claimed)	$ 25,604
The ANIMALS' AGENDA	$ 36,625	$ 22,427	$ 4,198
United Animal Nations	$ 34,710	$ 25,697	$ 2,844

NOTE

1. The figures for the American Humane Association are for the entire organization, since Form 990 data does not distinguish between assets of the child and animal protection divisions.

TABLE 3

ORGANIZATION	POSITION	PAY
Natl. Wildlife Federation	President	$200,000
The Nature Conservancy	President	$180,000
North Shore Animal League	Executive Director	$163,700
Humane Society of U.S.	President	$146,927
Natl. Audubon Society	President	$140,000
World Wildlife Fund	President	$133,881
Sierra Club Legal Defense Fund	Executive Director	$132,916
American SPCA	President	$130,819
Humane Society of U.S.	Treasurer	$123,301
African Wildlife Foundation	Executive Director	$122,000
The Wilderness Society	President	$120,000
Doris Day Animal League	Executive Director[1]	$110,440
Massachusetts SPCA	Dir., Rowley Hosp.	$106,188
World Wildlife Fund	Vice President	$105,225
World Wildlife Fund	Executive V.P.	$103,444
World Wildlife Fund	Chairman	$103,444
Defenders of Wildlife	President	$100,613
Massachusetts SPCA	Director of Pathology	$ 99,778
World Wildlife Fund	Consultant	$ 95,750
World Wildlife Fund	V.P. Planning	$ 95,454
Massachusetts SPCA	Director of Cardiology	$ 93,984
North Shore Animal League	Graphic Artist[2]	$ 90,000
Massachusetts SPCA	President	$ 89,706
World Wildlife Fund	Vice President	$ 88,875
Sierra Club	Executive Director	$ 86,000
Conservation International	President[3]	$ 85,000
AVERAGE SALARY OF ALL PAID U.S. CHARITY		
CHIEF EXECUTIVES[3]		**$ 83,000**
The Wilderness Society	Counselor	$ 85,000
North Shore Animal League	Director of Shelter	$ 82,950
North Shore Animal League	Veterinarian	$ 81,850
Massachusetts SPCA	Sr. Vice President	$ 80,440
American SPCA	Asst. Treasurer	$ 78,241
World Wildlife Fund	Vice President	$ 77,975
World Wildlife Fund	Vice President	$ 77,975
Humane Society of U.S.	Vice President	$ 77,567

172

TABLE 3 (continued)

ORGANIZATION	POSITION	PAY
American SPCA	Vice President	$ 77,544
Humane Society of U.S.	Vice President	$ 76,685
Massachusetts SPCA	Vice President	$ 76,317
Massachusetts SPCA	Director of Medicine	$ 75,796
American SPCA	Dispatcher	$ 75,570
Massachusetts SPCA	Director of Medicine	$ 74,067
American Humane Assn.	Secretary[4]	$ 73,359
World Wildlife Fund	Vice President	$ 72,525
AVERAGE SALARY OF PAID ANIMAL/HABITAT PROTECTION GROUP HEADS		**$ 71,199**
Humane Society of U.S.	Vice President	$ 71,063
Massachusetts SPCA	Vice President	$ 70,124
Natl. Humane Education Soc.	Fundraiser	$ 70,117
North Shore Animal League	Comptroller	$ 70,000
American Rivers	President	$ 70,000
Humane Society of U.S.	Vice President	$ 67,837
American SPCA	Sr. Vice President	$ 66,142
Humane Society of U.S.	Asst. Treasurer	$ 65,559
Animal Legal Defense Fund	Fundraiser	$ 65,329
Defenders of Wildlife	Editor	$ 64,983
Humane Society of U.S.	Vice President	$ 63,766
IFAW	CEO	$ 63,009
American SPCA	Foreperson	$ 61,538
American Humane Assn.	Child Protection[4]	$ 60,991
American Humane Assn.	Animal Protection	$ 60,741
Humane Society of U.S.	Vice President	$ 60,554
American SPCA	Sr. Investigator	$ 60,527
World Wildlife Fund	General Counsel	$ 60,184
Defenders of Wildlife	CEO	$ 59,614
ISAR	President	$ 59,000
Natl. Anti-Vivisection Society	Executive Director	$ 58,750
Natl. Anti-Vivisection Society	Attorney	$ 58,716
North Shore Animal League	Manager	$ 58,640
Defenders of Wildlife	Regional Director	$ 58,164
Defenders of Wildlife	Conservation Director	$ 57,055
Animal Protection Inst.	President	$ 55,621
United Action for Animals	President	$ 54,600

173

TABLE 3 (continued)

ORGANIZATION	POSITION	PAY
World Wildlife Fund	V.P. Finance	$ 54,394
Animal Protection Inst.	Consultant	$ 53,214
Natl. Humane Education Soc.	Consultant	$ 53,072
American Humane Assn.	Dir., Hollywood	$ 51,655
Defenders of Wildlife	Associate Director	$ 51,610
Humane Society of U.S.	Data Process. Director	$ 51,345
United Animal Nations	Comptroller	$ 50,845
United Action for Animals	Attorney/Lobbyist	$ 50,622
United Action for Animals	Research Director	$ 50,350
Connecticut Humane	Executive Director	$ 50,175
Friends of the Earth	President	$ 50,000
North Shore Animal League	Attorney	$ 49,467
Natl. Anti-Vivisection Society	President	$ 48,898
IFAW	Executive Director	$ 47,531
The Animals' Voice	Editor	$ 47,100
New Eng. Anti-Vivisection Soc.	Executive Director	$ 47,000
IFAW	Scientific Consultant	$ 46,480
United Animal Nations	Program Secretary	$ 46,266
Defenders of Wildlife	WLD Policy	$ 46,245
American Humane Assn.	Child Protection[4]	$ 45,883
IFAW	Public Relations	$ 45,514
American Anti-Vivisection Soc.	President	$ 44,682
American Humane Assn.	Dir., Wash., D.C.	$ 44,654
Natl. Anti-Vivisection Society	Consultant	$ 44,341
Massachusetts SPCA	Vice President	$ 43,979
In Defense of Animals	President	$ 43,920
Humane Society of U.S.	Dir. of Membership	$ 43,881
World Wildlife Fund	Asst. Secretary	$ 43,766
Animal Protection Inst.	(not stated)	$ 43,664
IFAW	Comptroller	$ 43,556
PETA	Dir. of Membership	$ 42,818
Humane Society of U.S.	Asst. Secretary	$ 42,758
Natl. Anti-Vivisection Society	Director	$ 42,650
Humane Society of U.S.	Govt. Relations	$ 42,141
Friends of Animals	President	$ 42,000
PETA	Executive Director	$ 41,000
Humane Society of U.S.	West Coast Dir.	$ 40,818

TABLE 3 (continued)

ORGANIZATION	POSITION	PAY
Humane Society of U.S.	Dir. of Higher Ed.	$ 40,249
PCRM	Dir. of Toxicology	$ 39,000
Animal Protection Inst.	(not stated)	$ 38,388
WLFA	VP/Treasurer	$ 38,763
Animal Protection Inst.	(not stated)	$ 38,078
The ANIMALS' VOICE	Director	$ 38,000
Humane Society of U.S.	Asst. Treasurer	$ 37,292
The ANIMALS' VOICE	Director	$ 36,400
Connecticut Humane	Financial Secretary	$ 36,120
Natl. Anti-Vivisection Society	Secretary	$ 36,050
Natl. Anti-Vivisection Society	Director Program/Educ.	$ 35,804
U.S. MEDIAN FAMILY INCOME		**$ 35,752**
American Humane Assn.	Asst. Secretary	$ 35,030
WFLA	President	$ 34,011
Greenpeace U.S.A.	Executive Director	$ 33,719
Friends of Animals	International Rep.	$ 33,000
Animal Protection Inst.	Consultant	$ 33,000
ISAR	Vice President	$ 33,000
Friends of Animals	Comptroller	$ 32,000
Animal Legal Defense Fund	Exec. Director	$ 31,600
Friends of Animals	Attorney	$ 31,500
Friends of Animals	New York Director	$ 31,500
PETA	Computers/Finance	$ 31,264
AVERAGE SALARY OF ANIMAL SHELTER DIRECTORS		**$ 31,236**
Animal Legal Defense Fund	Executive Director	$ 31,600
Humane Farming Assn.	Executive Director	$ 31,000
Animal Protection Inst.	Consultant	$ 30,959
The ANIMALS' VOICE	Director Asst.	$ 30,600
New Eng. Anti-Vivisection Soc.	Attorney	$ 30,560
PCRM	Communications	$ 30,423
PETA	Research/Investig.	$ 30,260
PETA	Dir./Communication	$ 30,237
The ANIMALS' VOICE	Director Asst.	$ 30,200
North Shore Animal League	Attorney	$ 30,000

TABLE 3 (continued)

IRS rules require that only the top five salaries within each organization need be reported. The following groups pay additional salaries in excess of $30,000:

North Shore Animal League (12)
Massachusetts SPCA (48)[5]
Humane Society of the U.S. (23)
American SPCA (72)

If a group pays no staff salaries above $30,000, the top five need not be declared. The following (in alphabetical order) pay no staff salaries above $30,000, and have not reported actual salaries:

Animal Welfare Institute
The Fund for Animals
The International Primate Protection League

ORGANIZATION	POSITION	PAY
Defenders of Animal Rights	President	$ 29,880
Defenders of Animal Rights	Vice President	$ 29,880
Natl. Humane Education Soc.	Vice President	$ 29,606
AVERAGE SALARY OF PAID SHELTER FUNDRAISING DIRECTORS		**$ 28,218**
PCRM	President	$ 28,000
Rainforest Action Network	Exec. Director	$ 28,000
Rainforest Alliance	Exec. Director	$ 26,248
American SPCA	Asst. Secretary	$ 26,113
Humane Farming Assn.	Treasurer/Secretary	$ 26,500
The ANIMALS' AGENDA	Circulation Dir.	$ 23,000
The ANIMALS' AGENDA	Editor	$ 22,995
The ANIMALS' AGENDA	Advertising Dir.	$ 22,995
Massachusetts SPCA	Vice President	$ 22,687
AVERAGE SALARY OF PAID SHELTER PUBLIC RELATIONS OFFICERS		**$ 21,500**
In Defense of Animals	Director[6]	$ 21,100
AVERAGE SALARY OF PAID SHELTER MANAGERS		**$ 21,025**
PETA	Chairman	$ 21,000
AVERAGE SALARY OF PAID FULL-TIME HUMANE EDUCATORS		**$ 20,500**
American Anti-Vivisection Soc.	Vice President	$ 19,038
Earth Island Inst.	Exec. Director	$ 18,794
The ANIMALS' AGENDA	Editor-at-Large	$ 18,220
Adopt-A-Pet	Exec. Director	$ 18,000
AVERAGE SALARY OF ANIMAL CRUELTY OFFICERS		**$ 17,300**
Earth Island Inst.	Exec. Director	$ 17,227

176

TABLE 3 (continued)

ORGANIZATION	POSITION	PAY
Trans-Species Unlimited	President	$ 15,000
Trans-Species Unlimited	Treasurer	$ 15,000
Adopt-A-Pet	Attorney	$ 14,445
American Anti-Vivisection Soc.	Secretary	$ 14,143
The ANIMALS' AGENDA	News Editor	$ 13,960
AVERAGE SALARY OF PAID ANIMAL SHELTER STAFFERS		**$ 13,019**
ISAR	Asst. Secretary	$ 8,906
ISAR	Vice President	$ 8,625
Primarily Primates	President	$ 6,000
American SPCA	Asst. Secretary	$ 5,508
Adopt-A-Pet	President	$ 4,555
Farm Sanctuary	President	$ 2,598
Farm Sanctuary	Vice President	$ 2,598
Farm Sanctuary	Treasurer	$ 2,598
American Anti-Vivisection Soc.	Treasurer	$ 1,584
Natl. Humane Education Soc.	President	(living quarters)
The Fund for Animals	President	None
Earth Island Institute	Chairman of Board	None
SUPRESS	Founder/Director	None
AVAR	President	None
Com. for Humane Legislation	President[7]	None
Earth First!	Founder	None
FARM	President	None
IPPL	Chairwoman	None
The Animals' Voice	Publisher	None
United Animal Nations	Secretary General	None
PETA	Natl. Director	None
The Fund for Animals	Secretary	None
Animal Welfare Institute	President	None
Ducks Unlimited	President	None
Sea Shepherd Conservation Soc.	Captain	None

NOTES

1. It was reported in *The Animals' Agenda* that the Executive Director "receives no salary from the Doris Day Animal League, but as a note appended to the group's Form 990 explains, 'The law firm of Galvin, Stanley, and Hazard provides to the League legislative representation, public education, and executive management services through a partner

177

in its firm who functions as the League's Executive Director. . . Expenses to Galvin, Stanley, and Hazard amounted to $110,440 in 1989. . .' Form 990 data indicates $69,536 was paid for accounting, $56,475 for public relations help, and $28,898 for legal services other than those provided by [incumbent]."

2. *The Animals' Agenda* reported that the incumbent is "affiliated with" a group of the same name as his, "which supplies finished mechanicals for mailing packages to the North Shore Animal League (NSAL), subject to NSAL's review and approval. On the basis of a written agreement, the. . . group was paid $50,000 in 1989."

3. This information comes from the American Society of Association Executives. By locale, chief executives in Washington, D.C. average $121,368; in New York, $111,373; and in Chicago, $109,253.

4. According to *The Animals' Agenda,* the chief executive officers of the American Humane Association preside over both animal and child protection programs. Two officers work exclusively in child protection.

5. Approximately half of the Massachusettrs SPCA salaries that exceed $30,000 go to veterinarians at Angell Memorial Hospital.

6. According to *The Animals' Agenda,* the incumbent was paid by both In Defense of Animals ($21,100) and ISAR ($8,625) in 1989, but was no longer with ISAR in 1990.

7. According to *The Animals' Agenda,* the incumbent is also President of Friends of Animals, earning $42,000 a year.

Suggested Further Reading

Amory, Cleveland. *Man Kind? Our Incredible War on Wildlife*. New York: Harper and Row, 1974.
This classic shows that nice people don't hunt.

Barnard, Neal. *The Power of the Plate*. Summertown, TN: Summertown Book Publishing Co., 1990.
A leading physician demonstrates that animal products are not only unnecessary but are harmful to the human diet.

Fox, Michael W. *Inhumane Society: The American Way of Exploiting Animals*. New York: St. Martin's Press, 1990.
In the words of Ingrid Newkirk, this is "a compelling indictment of the veterinary community and other animal industries."

Kotzwinkle, William. *Doctor Rat*. New York: Avon Books, 1971.
A chilling satire of vivisection.

Lofting, Hugh. *Dr. Doolittle*. Philadelphia: J. B. Lippincott, 1948.
This classic fairy tale illustrates how animals anticipate and feel pain.

Mason, Jim, and Peter Singer. *Animal Factories*. New York: Crown, 1980.
After reading this book, you may never consume dairy products again.

McKenna, Virginia. *Beyond the Bars*. Wellingborough, Northamptonshire, England: Thorsun's, 1987.
After reading this book, you may never patronize a zoo again.

Newkirk, Ingrid. *Save the Animals! 101 Easy Things You Can Do*. New York: Warner Books, 1990.
This is the best practical guide for helping animals that has ever been written.

Orwell, George. *Animal Farm*. New York: Harcourt and Brace, 1946.
This classic satire shows how animals view factory farming.

Regan, Tom. *The Case for Animal Rights*. Berkeley, CA: University of California Press, 1984.
> This book is "must" reading for anyone who enters into debates on the issues of animals' rights.

Robbins, John. *Diet for a New America*. Walpole, NJ: Stillpoint, 1987.
> Read this book and you will become a vegetarian, if you are not one already.

Schwartz, Richard H. *Judaism and Vegetarianism*. Marblehead, MA: Micah Publications (Jews for Animal Rights), 1988.
> This book resolves perceived conflicts between the Old Testament and animals' rights.

Sharpe, Robert. *The Cruel Deception*. Wellingborough, Northamptonshire, England: Thorsun's, 1988.
> A physician presents irrefutable evidence proving that the use of animals in medical research is hazardous to human nature.

Singer, Peter. *Animal Liberation*. New York: New York Review, 1990.
> This is the second edition to Peter Singer's 1975 book that started it all.

Spiegel, Marjorie. *The Dreaded Comparison*. New York: Mirror Books, 1990.
> In the words of Alice Walker, author of *The Color Purple*: "Marjorie Spiegel illustrates the similarities between the enslavement of black people in the past and the enslavement of animals, past and present."

Townsend, Virginia. *Pulling the Wool!* Sydney, Australia: Hale and Iremonger, 1985.
> This book reveals the cruelty of the "harvesting" of wool.

RECOMMENDED MAGAZINES:

The Animals' Agenda, 456 Monroe Turnpike, Monroe, CT 06468; tel. (203) 452-0446

The Animals' Voice Magazine, P.O. Box 16955, N. Hollywood, CA 91615; tel. (213) 204-2323

Vegetarian Times, P.O. Box 570, Oak Park, IL 60303; tel. (708) 848-8100